i

Isabella Murray Wright

STIRLING LETTERS

By

ISABELLA MURRAY WRIGHT
(1846-1932)

written in 1894 at 26 Victoria Place, Stirling

For my dear Isobel and Leslie, a book of "Auntie's" Memories. Being Chronicles of the Murray and Wright Families over the period of 150 years.

Transcribed by Sue Jamieson

Published with sponsorship from

THE POST OFFICE

and

The Russell Trust

ACKNOWLEDGMENTS

The Trustees and Friends of the Smith Art Gallery and Museum are indebted to Mrs Elizabeth Burns (the daughter of Isobel Haldane Murray Campbell, for whom this book was written) and her family. Although this is a privately owned family journal, it is in many ways a social history of central Scotland for the period 1745-1894, and in recognition of its historical importance, Mrs Burns and her family have allowed it to be published. Her son Alasdair Monro has provided a family tree to illustrate the relationships mentioned in the book.

The publication would not have been possible without the dedicated hard work of Sue Jamieson of the Friends of the Smith, who between 1993 and 1997 transcribed the manuscript with the utmost care, and undertook research into the life of the author. Additional research on the paintings of Jane Ann Wright (1842-1922) in the Smith's collections, was undertaken by Evelyn Paton.

Many Friends of the Smith have helped with this publication in different ways. John Scott and Margaret Duff read the typescript and made many helpful suggestions.

Special thanks go to Eunice Wyles for allowing us to quote from her poem, to Bob McCutcheon for access to his reference collection and to Peter Campbell for the accurate transcription of the Gaelic song on page 117.

Typing and text management were undertaken by Moira Anderson of Central Regional Council, and Hilary O'Donnell of the Stirling Smith. Additional help with the information technology was given by Terry O'Donnell. Editing, footnotes and index were produced by Elspeth King.

Christopher Steward and his team at Stirling Reprographics worked tirelessly to produce a good book for Stirling.

Martin Cummins of the Post Office was quick to recognise the historical value of the journal and persuade his Board to sponsor the publication. A grant from the Russell Trust enabled the production of a better quality book.

The Stirling Smith Art Gallery and Museum is an independent Scottish Charity, SCO16162, serving the Stirling area, and funded by Stirling Council, with the support of its Friends, the business community, and private trusts and foundations.

Charles Broadfoot
Chairman, Smith Trustees

The Burns-Tilley-Monro family would like to say a special "thank you" to Elspeth King, whose idea it was to publish these writings, and to Sue Jamieson, who undertook the tremendous work of transcribing them. Their enthusiasm and hard work made it easy for us to share our family with them. We hope now that other people too may be interested in these memories of Scotland long ago, and that the Smith Art Gallery and Museum should benefit would certainly please the author.

Elizabeth Burns

ISBN 0 9525332 51
FIRST PUBLISHED 1998

by the

Stirling Smith Art Gallery and Museum
Dumbarton Road
Stirling FK8 2RQ
museum@smithartgallery.demon.co.uk

Printed and bound by **Stirling Reprographics.**

CONTENTS

LIST OF ILLUSTRATIONS

FOREWORD

The desire to peep into the lives of others, especially when they belong to a past to which time gives an ever more elegant patina, is something most of us find irresistible.

These 'Chronicles' of the Murray and Wright families provide a delightful record of times past for those living a 'privileged' life style here in Stirling and London. They also have fascinating asides: tea being a luxury at 7/6d a pound; servants calling their aprons a "brat"; the "sweetmeat" rock, be it of the Stirling or Edinburgh variety all having "Gibraltar" rock as their common predecessor; and Miss Murray finding the Duke of Wellington a "small, insignificant man in a plain, dark uniform."

For The Post Office and support of this book, the connection is obvious. The role of the letter in the lives of those whose lives fill the pages of this book is all important. After the great reforms (1840) of Sir Rowland Hill, whose concept of mail being charged by weight not distance, is still a cornerstone of Royal Mail policy, people could look back, as Isabella Wright does in 1894, to the previous high postage. A letter from Glasgow to Edinburgh cost 7d in 1835 and one from Glasgow to London 1/1d

The Chronicles also have a vivid but nostalgic reference to pre-railway days when mail was carried 'on horseback or in carts' and to July 7 1788, in particular, when the London mail arrived at the Saracen's Head, Glasgow, "surrounded by a crowd of horsemen who had ridden out to meet it."

A little over 100 years on from "auntie" Isabella Murray Wright's Chronicles, The Post Office continues to play a major part in the social and business life of Stirling, Scotland and further afield. Despite the digital age, the postie's rattle of the letter box and the country's post offices, which nearly three and a half million Scots visit each week, remain valued personal experiences in an age of increasing impersonality.

Finally, we would like to congratulate Elspeth King and the Stirling Smith Art Gallery and Museum for bringing this book to the attention of the many.

JOHN WARD, CBE

Chairman, Scottish Post Office Board

INTRODUCTION

In February 1894, at the age of 48, Isabella Murray Wright sat down to write a personal letter to her two small nieces, explaining the family background. She does not say how long she took, but she filled 247 pages of a notebook in black ink, with no corrections or changes of direction, in a hand which flows as easily as her prose style. The document, which contains copies of many other family letters, extends to 64,000 words. The story of each branch of the family is chronicled in succession, down to the birth and babyhood of her two nieces.

As the letter was not meant for general publication, some editing has been done, and explanatory notes have been added, especially in respect of material in the Stirling Smith's collections.

This long letter is very much a Stirling book. Isabella was writing from her house in Victoria Place, in the gracious King's Park suburb of Stirling, not far from the Stirling Smith Art Gallery and Museum. Although Isabella and her sisters were born and brought up in St Vincent Street, Glasgow, most of the family ties were in the Stirling area, and on the death of her father in 1860, Isabella and her family moved to 7 Park Terrace in Stirling. In 1887, they moved again to 26 Victoria Place. She and her sister Jane Anne Wright remained unmarried and in the great tradition of the Scottish maiden aunts were devoted to their nieces Isobel and Leslie, the daughters of their sister Mary. Isabella wrote stories for her nieces, some of which were printed in local newspapers. Jane Anne was an artist of some talent, interested in history and antiquities, and the Stirling Smith owns 81 of her watercolour drawings of Stirlingshire houses and mansions. Her obituary in 1922 describes her as 'a modern edition of Scott's "Jonathan Oldbuck"' (the principal character in The Antiquary) who surrounded herself with relics of the past, many of them of great antiquarian interest'.

There are many branches of the Murray family in Stirlingshire, and Isabella records visits to many different Murray households - Polmaise, Livilands, Murrayshall, and the various town houses. Of principal interest was Livilands, the house of her grandparents. Parts of this house were medieval, and when the staircase to the feature which she describes as the 'Eagle's Hole' was removed, an important painted panelled scheme, dating from the 17th century and featuring the Sybils, the female prophetesses of antiquity, was discovered. The panelling was given to the national museums and will go on public display for the first time when the new Museum of Scotland opens in November 1998. Isabella does not mention the panels probably because there were other accounts of them she had already written for the local newspapers. The grounds of Livilands are now occupied by Stirling Royal Infirmary.

It was Isabella's grandfather, John Murray, who built the first house in what is now Melville Terrace in about 1807, and started a fashion for grand houses on the south and west side of Stirling. The development of the Victorian suburb of King's Park, on the site of the old hunting ground of the Stuart kings, was speeded up with the coming of the railway in 1848, enabling those who made their money in industrial Glasgow, to live in the clean environment of Stirling.

The value of Isabella's letter or journal lies in the word picture she paints of the network of Stirlingshire families, Jacobite by politics and tradition and related by marriage, who worshipped together in the Scottish Episcopal Church. The curate in Stirling, Bishop Gleig had played a part in securing the repeal of the Penal Laws which had prohibited their worship, and the first Episcopal Church in Stirling was built shortly afterwards.

Most of the families in this circle - the Murrays of Polmaise and Livilands, the Stirlings of Keir, Kippendavie and Garden, the Moirs of Leckie, the Wordies of Cambusbarron, the Seton Stuarts of Touch, and the MacGregors of Balhadie - had helped the cause of Prince Charles Edward Stuart in 1745/6 when he came to lead a Jacobite army and claim the throne for his father. It was from the strength of the Jacobite landed gentry of Stirlingshire that Prince Charles Edward Stuart drew his support in the lowlands. Some paid dearly for it. Buchanan of Arnprior and Lennie was executed and his lands forfeited; the MacGregors had to change their very name.

While these family networks lasted into the 19th and 20th centuries, they were not monolithic. Isabella Murray Wright's father was a cotton broker, and the friends of the family in Glasgow were industrialists of similar standing, involved in textiles and engineering. The MacDowalls of Castle Semple and the Wrights of Calder Park, both in Renfrewshire and related by marriage to the Murrays, also made their money from textiles.

Although the main narrative centres on the family, many people of national significance feature in the text - the songwriter Lady Caroline Oliphant of Gask, the novelist Mrs Grant of Laggan, various members of the royal family, Dr Thomas Chalmers who led the Disruption in 1843, and the tragic Dr Edward Irving.

The economic and political dimensions are missing from Isabella Murray Wright's book, but such background is available in countless standard histories. The greatest value of her letters is that she concentrates on domestic and family life, describing the ordinary and the commonplace, and writing about issues which economic and political historians regard as being of no significance.

The details she provides of births, childhood, schooling, illness, marriage, death, and mourning, create for us, through her eyes, a very full picture of her past. She tells us about the contents of ladies' pockets, and of how a proper wash day was conducted. Essentially, it is a woman's perspective of the past, written for two women of the future, and thanks to her skills as a writer, and eye for detail, there is information in the book which cannot fail to delight, surprise and inform the reader.

As with other Scottish towns, the history of Stirling has often been written as the history of Stirling's men, and the public face of the town in respect of statues and street names is uncompromisingly male. Eunice Wyles' poem *The Forgotten Women of Stirling* aptly sums this up:

> Immortalised in stane and bronze;
> heroic Bruce and Wallace guard
> their battlefields at ilka turns,
> Rob Roy brandishes his dirk
> at the back o' Rabbie Burns..
> stane tributes raised in national pride,
> for statesman, sodger, cotter -
> every yin, a Scottish son
> but nane for ony Scottish dochter:
> an' a' the streets hae names o' men,
> Cowane, Gladstone, Pitt;
> Parks and Shops an' Businesses
> assume a national plebesite -
> a world o' men, by men created,
> nae hilt nor hair o' weemen seen

This book will go some way towards providing a much needed women's perspective on Stirling's history.

Many ladies of Isabella's generation and before, kept diaries, commonplace books and journals. Another notable example in Stirling is the diary of Helen Graham (1805-1896), daughter of the Governor of Stirling Castle, written in the years 1823-1826 and published under the title 'Parties and Pleasures' in 1956.

Edith Holden (1871-1920) whose journal became world famous when published as *The Country Diary of an Edwardian Lady* in 1977 also came to Stirling to study art under Joseph Denovan Adam. Stirling men, such as J W Campbell of Glentirran, Isabella's brother in law, and David B Morris, Town Clerk, also published their reminiscences, but such accounts are quite rare.

What makes Isabella's book important is the intimacy of the narrative and the fact that she is acting as a kind of museum curator of the family 'treasures' or material culture. Families are notorious for discarding the possessions of elderly relatives after the funeral. In the Murray-Wright-Burns-Monro family, which has a strong sense of history, such mistakes are not made.

Much of Isabella's narrative is focused on and is a celebration of these objects - a spoon, a bowl, a piece of sheet, the homespun cloth, and the spinning wheel which produced it. Napery, wedding china, christening gifts and family toys are lovingly described, as are the family portraits, jewellery, and Jacobite relics owned by different branches of the family. Each one of them unlocks for her a family story, a memory of shared experience, a part of the past, and with her journal, she is documenting the objects as a means of transmitting family history. Isabella had the insight to recognise in those objects regardless of their monetary worth, their historical and talismanic value as a touchstone of human history, common to our collective past. Objects similar to these comprise the content of Scotland's museum collections today, and those in her writings are the stuff of Stirling's history. For these reasons, the Stirling Smith is pleased to publish this work.

Elspeth King

Stirling Smith Art Gallery and Museum

Scene in Torbrex House. The Engagement of Isabelle Haldane Murray Campbell, one of the girls for whom this book is written. Her adoring aunts and other relatives admire her ring, while the family dog longs for peace!

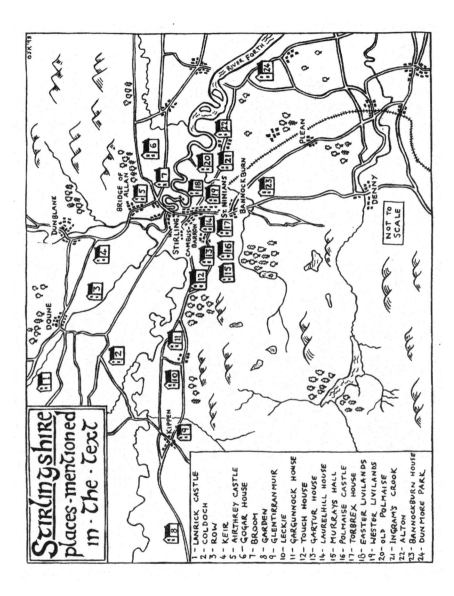

Stirlingshire
places·mentioned
in·the·Text

1 – LANRICK CASTLE
2 – COLDOCH
3 – ROW
4 – KEIR
5 – AIRTHREY CASTLE
6 – GOGAR HOUSE
7 – BROOM
8 – GARDEN
9 – GLENTIRRAN MUIR
10 – LECKIE
11 – GARGUNNOCK HOUSE
12 – TOUCH HOUSE
13 – GARTUR HOUSE
14 – LAURELHILL HOUSE
15 – MURRAYS HALL
16 – POLMAISE CASTLE
17 – TORBREX HOUSE
18 – EASTER LIVILANDS
19 – WESTER LIVILANDS
20 – OLD POLMAISE
21 – INGRAM'S CROOK
22 – ALTON
23 – BANNOCKBURN HOUSE
24 – DUNMORE PARK

NOT TO SCALE

RIVER FORTH
BRIDGE OF ALLAN
DUNBLANE
DOUNE
KIPPEN
STIRLING
CAMBUS-BARRON
St NINIANS
PLEAN
BANNOCKBURN
DENNY

OJK '98

PLACES MENTIONED IN THE TEXT

Allanton	Estate in the Parish of Cambusnethan, Lanarkshire, near Shotts, with elegant mansion house
Ardchullarie	Farmhouse on the east side of Loch Lubnaig in the Trossachs
Bannockburn House	Built in 1674 with 18th and 19th century additions; it is south of Bannockburn near the junction of the A91 and A872
Balhadie	Hamlet in the Ardoch district of the Parish of Dunblane
Braehead	Farm on Polmaise and Touchadam Estate, no longer standing
Brentham Park	A Victorian mansion built in 1871, adjacent to Wester Livilands House, still standing today
Broom House	On the north bank of the River Forth, still extant, about one mile east of Stirling
Coldoch House	Situated between Blair Drummond and Thornhill, to the north west of Stirling
Craig	Estate and mansion in Kilmaurs parish, Ayrshire, 4 miles WSW of Kilmarnock
Croy	Large estate, south of the Blane, western edge of the Parish of Killearn, now a village near Cumbernauld
Dunmore Park	Built for the 5th Earl of Dunmore between 1820 and 1822 to the designs of William Wilkins, adjacent to the "Pineapple", nine and a half miles north west of Airth. Now derelict
Garden House	Built in 1824, this classical 19th century mansion house, in the style of David Hamilton lies north of the A811, Stirling to Dumbarton road, ten miles west of Stirling
Gargunnock House	A fine H-shaped 18th century mansion house just over half a mile east of the village of Gargunnock, six miles west of Stirling, off the A811 Stirling to Dumbarton road

Gartur House	An early 19th century Regency mansion, still standing about two and a half miles west of Stirling, one mile south of Cambusbarron. Now derelict
Glentirran House	Adjacent to the hamlet of Glentirranmuir, about one mile east of Kippen, this property is no longer standing
Gogar House	A two-storey mid 18th century house south of the A91 Stirling to St Andrews road, three miles east of Stirling
Ingram's Crook	Farmhouse and steading on the lands of Touchadam and Polmaise, now no longer standing. Land redeveloped as industrial estate north of the A905 towards Grangemouth
Lanrick Castle	Standing on the south bank of the River Teith, two and a half miles west of Doune and 11 miles north west of Stirling, just off the A84 Stirling to Callander road, this seat of the Haldanes was castellated and turretted in 1791. Now derelict.
Laurelhill House	Standing near the junction of King's Park Road and Park Place, Stirling, it was built in 1806 and was typical of the period. It was demolished in 1973 and forms the site of Laurelhill Business Park and new housing development
Leckie House	A restored 16th century T-shaped laird's house, about two and a half miles east of Kippen, about seven miles west of Stirling, on the A811 Stirling to Dumbarton road
Watson House	Formerly New Leckie, a splendid Jacobean mansion adjacent to Leckie House.
Easter Livilands House	Lying in St Ninians Parish, it was demolished in the 1960s to allow the construction of a new private housing scheme, Pelstream Avenue and Melfort Drive
Wester Livilands House	The original 17th century mansion house was replaced in 1898 by a new building, which today forms Westerlands Nursing Home, adjacent to Clifford Road and Brentham Crescent, Stirling
Monreith	Estate and mansion in the parish of Mochrum, south west of Wigtown, in Dumfries and Galloway district

Murrays Hall	Built in 1673 by the Laird of Touchadam, about two miles south west of Stirling, it was totally destroyed by quarrying operations in the 20th century
Old Polmaise	Built in the 17th century (1697) on the banks of the River Forth near Fallin, it is now derelict
Polmaise Castle	Built in 1865 in the Fir Park above Cambusbarron, it was vacated by the Murray family in 1956. The ruins became dangerous and were demolished in 1966
Row House	A two-storey building, built in 1862, it still stands on the north side of the River Teith, two miles south west of Doune
Touch House	Situated at the foot of the Touch Hills, around three kilometres west of Stirling and about half a mile south of the A811 Stirling to Dumbarton road, it is dominated by the Georgian south front. It is still standing
Torbrex House	Built in 1721, it is now The Inn in the Torbrex district of Stirling

The Royal Burgh of Stirling

Dear Isobel and Leslie,

Auntie Jean has made so many genealogical trees, both of the Murrays and the Wrights, that it is needless for me to recapitulate them here. You will see from them, that we have, on both sides "a lang pedigree." So I shall not go further back than Alexander Murray, who was a Lieutenant in the 22nd Regiment, born July 7th 1737, died June 25th 1777. He married Isabel Wordie, daughter of John Wordie of Cambusbarron. She is the old lady, whose picture hangs in our drawing room, whom you children, have always known as "Old Isobel." When you were a baby, my Isobel, Grannie used to say to you when you cried, "O stop, stop, look at old Isobel, she's looking at you, and she never cries" and you would stop suddenly, and look at the picture, and say solemnly, "no, never kies." But in her time, old Isobel, good, brave, woman, must have shed many tears, for she had her sorrows. Her husband died young, leaving her with three children, William, John and Christian. William, a cadet in the East Indian Company's Service died at Calcutta May 11th 1717, to the great grief of his mother and his many friends. He seems to have been greatly beloved, and was very handsome. So, too, was his brother John, my grandfather, born August 17th 1774. There is a silhouette of the two brothers at Row, which Jane-Anne copied carefully for ourselves, representing them with long pigtails (I think they were called "queues") and lace cravats. This is the only likeness there is of William, and how often his mother must have looked lovingly at it, she who cherished his letters so carefully, these letters which we now have!

JEAN BUCHANAN OF CROY AND JOHN MURRAY

John, our grandfather, married December 1st 1807, Jean Buchanan of Croy, born Tuesday July 29th 1783 an orphan, and ward of her kinsman, Mr. Buchanan of Dowanhill.[1] Their married life was very happy. She had a very bright, merry disposition. She was slight, with dark hair, and small hands, and fingers so tapered, and with such exquisitely formed nails, that Mother said they used to make her unclose her hands so that they might admire them. Old Mrs. Stirling of Garden, told me once when we were at Garden that Aunt Duthie resembled her father and Mother her mother. Mrs. Pollock -Morris told me Jean was devoted to her husband, and would hail all his remarks and jokes with delight. "O John, John" she would say, in fits of merry laughter.

In after years, Mrs. Morris said when she stayed with our grandfather, there was a change; for Jean was then lying restfully in the Polmaise vault in the old churchyard of St. Ninians. Jean of the tiny hands and tapered fingers, and the merry voice, and her successor, Ann McGregor of Balhaldie, a very

---

1   Glasgow. Dowanhill House was situated in the area now bordered by Dowanhill, Hyndland, Lawrence and White Streets, and featured on maps until 1900.

John Murray (1774-1861) of Livilands

stately dame, possibly as devoted to her husband as was Jean, but very correct and proper, did not appreciate jokes. And so it was no longer, "O John, John!" and a merry laugh, but "O Murray, how can you!" Mrs. Morris used always to end her stories of our grandfather, by saying, "he was a dear old man, a dear old man, and so fond of me!"

Our grandmother, Jean Buchanan, was the last of her family, all died young, except herself and her brother Lapsley. He made several voyages abroad, possibly on account of his health. The box of foreign shells, now in my possession, was brought home by him to his sister Jean. He was 25 or 26 years old when he died.

Jean lived with her guardian, Mr Buchanan, and her governess's name was Miss Taylor. At one time, her lessons were shared by her cousin, Agnes Whitehead, afterwards Mrs. Macnaughton, whose parents lived at Cowie,[2] now a farm, then a distillery near Bannockburn, and it was there that our grandfather fell in love with Jean, when she was visiting her aunt, Mrs Whitehead.

MARRIAGE OF JOHN MURRAY AND JEAN BUCHANAN

They were married at Crookston Castle,[3] near Paisley, where her guardian lived before he bought Dowanhill near Glasgow. And by an odd coincidence, dear Isobel and Leslie, they, your great grandparents on your mother's side, were married by Doctor William Porteous of Glasgow, your great, great grandfather on your father's side. Jean was a bright merry girl full of life and vivacity. On one occasion, when she and Miss Taylor had ridden from Glasgow, and were resting their ponies at Stirling, on their way to Croy, she heard that there was to be a dance in the Guildhall.[4] Thither they went, riding habit not withstanding, and danced gaily. I think Agnes Whitehead her cousin, was there too.

I have heard old Miss Nancy Lucas, Mrs. Whitehead's granddaughter, say that when our grandfather was shooting near Cowie, and meant to dine there, he always fired off his gun at a certain place, to give notice of his intention, whereupon Mrs Whitehead would say to her cook, 'put on the beef and greens, Mr Murray is coming to dinner'. I think he must always have had very kindly feeling for Cowie for it was there he courted his bonnie Jean.

2   Cowie, parish of St Ninians, to the south of Stirling. Distillery licensees: Jane Buchanan 1795, Mrs Whitehead 1798-9, James McNab 1817-28. In ruins by 1860. A farm by 1894.

3   Now ruinous, it is a scheduled Ancient Monument in the care of Historic Scotland.

4   The popular name for Cowane's Hospital, beside the Church of the Holy Rude, St John Street. Dances are still held there.

Melville Place from the rear c1880
Watercolour sketch by Jane Anne Wright

FASHIONS IN NAMES

He took her home to the house he had built, Melville Place,[5] and there on December 31st, 1808 their eldest child, Mary, was born. She was christened Mary, after Jean's mother, Mary Hutton (Mrs Buchanan). Our own dear mother was born October 1st 1810, and christened Isabella Wordie, by Bishop Gleig. She was named after her father's mother, and ought to have been Isobel; but there is a fashion in names as in everything else, and Isobel was beginning to be thought antiquated. So much so, that our great grandmother began to sign her name "Isabella", and our grandmother Jean, became "Jane"! And now (1894) for some years, the wheel of fashion has again turned, and all the Janes who want to be fashionable, are again Jeans, the Isabellas, Isobels, and there are Dorothys, Barbaras, Marjories ad libitum. So fluctuating a thing is fashion!

There are few now living in Stirling who were baptised by Bishop Gleig. Mother and old John Lickrish were the oldest, and they used to be very proud to say that they were the oldest baptised members in the church. "You, Lickrish", Mother would say, "are the father, and I am the mother of the Church." Mrs Dalgetty and Mrs Gardiner in Baker Street, sisters whose maiden name was Spittal,[6] were also baptised by Bishop Gleig, but they were younger. Dear Mother and Mr Dalgetty are gone, but Lickrish and Mrs Gardiner still live (1894).

Our grandparent's third child, Alexander, was born in 1812, and there were great rejoicings that it was a boy, our grandfather being heir-presumptive to Polmaise.

THE SUTHERLAND BOWL OR "SILVER CUP"

There was a certain eccentric old lady, Mrs Sutherland, (known by the name of Lady Woodie, because she had once lived at Gartur, then called Woodend) who was a great friend of my grandfather's. She possessed a silver punch bowl, called 'the silver cup', with the Sutherland crest on it, and my grandfather used to brew punch in it, and called it 'the wicked little bowl'. He laughingly said to Mrs Sutherland, "if the child is a boy, give him the silver cup." A short time after the child was born, (only an hour or two, I think) "Lady Woodie" crept noiselessly upstairs, and finding the nurse had left the room, ran in, drew aside the bed curtains of the four poster bed where Jean lay, threw in the bowl, saying "hae, that's for the laddie", and departed as quickly as she came. This silver bowl, dear Isobel and Leslie, lies with the other silver things on the old spinning wheel table in our drawing room.

JENNY MCNAB

A fourth child, Jane, was born in December, 1814 and died when she was 13 months old, January 1816. She was buried in the burying ground of the Wordies of Cambusbarron in the old Churchyard of St Ninians.[7] Mother and I hunted about for the Wordies' resting place but the stones are defaced. The place where she though it was, is just outside the old Church Tower, on the side farthest away from Stirling. Nine years after this baby's birth, the youngest child Christian Jane, was born on June 27th, 1823. The faithful and devoted nurse of these children, the only nurse they ever had, was Jenny McNab. She must have been an excellent woman in every way. Though she did not like the second Mrs Murray, she stayed on for love of her nurslings, and it was to Jenny they went to for sympathy. Indeed, Mother said, they infinitely preferred the nursery to the drawing room; and sometimes when all sorts of fun was going on there, they would hear their stepmother come out from the drawing room, and pause a moment as if to listen, and then go away. They did not invite her up, they were happiest with Jenny, poor young things; and she, not unnaturally was jealous of their love for Jenny.

---

5   Now No 3 Melville Terrace, Stirling, headquarters of the Freight Transport Association.

6   The Spittals were an important family in Stirling. Robert Spittal, tailor to James V, built Spittals Hospital as a poors house in 1530. The building still stands in Spittal Street.

7   The church in the village of St Ninians was accidentally blown up by the Jacobite Army in 1746. Only the tower was left standing. The burial ground remained in use.

But this is a digression. I must go back to the life at Melville Place in my own grandmother's time. Stirling must have been very different then to what it is now. Melville Place was, I think, the first house built there. There was, of course, no Park Terrace,[8] and when Mr. Sconce built his house there, it was thought a most absurd and dreary place to build in. This house now belongs to Mr. Galbraith, the Town Clerk (1894). Port Street, so called because of the Port or gate which used to be there [9](old people even now call it "the Port") had old fashioned houses on both sides, some with red tiled roofs.

"LADY WOODIE" - OLD STIRLING IN 1809

Mrs. Sutherland, Lady Woodie, lived where Carson,[10] the painter, now is. There she died. She always wore a black silk bonnet, in fact, she was never seen without it, and she wore it on her deathbed. One of her oddities was, that she declared no-one should ever see her die! And she kept her word; for when she felt her end drawing near, she told her maid to draw the curtains close round the bed and leave her alone. This, awestruck maid did. But as time went on, hours, I think and, silence reigned, she parted the curtains, and looked in, and was greeted with "Ye aye had a d—- lot of impudence." So she drew the curtains again, and waited. Next time she peeped in all was over. And so "Lady Woodie's" soul went out into the darkness.

I heard Mother tell this story of Mrs. Sutherland to someone when I was a very little child, so young that she probably never thought I would understand it, but it made a great impression on me; and I used to wonder where Lady Woodie went after making such a speech. It filled me with awe. And yet, and yet, who knows what she thought as she lay there alone. We are not the judges. The great Dr Chalmers[11] spoke truly when he said that those of us who get to heaven would no doubt be much astonished at the people we should find there, and the people we should miss.

---

8   First properties built to follow Legate's feuing plan in King's Park 1834. Original houses, No 32 Park Lodge built by Sheriff R Sconce, 29-31 inclusive by Mr R Haldane, 1-7 market garden owned by Mr A Abercrombie. Few houses until rapid development post 1853-54 when gas lamps installed. 28 houses in place by 1860.

9   The site of the town's main gate. At junction with Dumbarton Road, in the ground is a plaque marking the site of the Port from which it takes it name.

10 Business address then 58 Port Street. Building replaced by distinctive three storey Queen Anne style building in 1901.

11 Reverend Dr Thomas Chalmers (1780-1847) who led the Disruption of 1843 which created the Free Church of Scotland.

The Episcopal Chapel Stirling, interior and exterior.
Watercolours by Jane Anne Wright, Smith Art Gallery and Museum

The Esplanade at the Castle[12] was made in 1809. Between it and the old Churchyard, where the cemetery now is, was called "the Valley",[13] and there all sorts of travelling shows used to exhibit. It was a common thing for one to say to another "the fules (i.e. fools) have come", or "are you going to see the fules in the Valley?"

BISHOP GLEIG 1787-1840, JENNY WELSH

The original Episcopal chapel,[14] as it was called, stood on that three cornered bit of ground, opposite the Royal Hotel, at the end of Barnton Street, where a high block of buildings now is. Before it was built, in the time of the Penal Laws, Episcopalians worshipped God in an "upper room" in Broad Street. Mr. Gleig, the late Chaplain General of the Forces, remembered being taken there as a child. But these cruel laws were repealed, and the new Chapel built. It was served by Bishop Gleig, Bishop of Brechin, who held the incumbency of Stirling. (Appointed to Stirling in 1787. Consecrated Bishop 1808. Died March 9 1840)[15]

He lived in a house in Upper Bridge Street,[16] then an old fashioned locality, with his stepdaughter, Miss Janet Fulton. Jenny Welsh, our dear Jenny, was his housemaid for seven years, and the cook was Peggy, Mrs. Morrison, a widow, mother of Margaret Morrison (now Mrs. Macarthur, Glenaray Schoolhouse) who was our table maid in St. Vincent Street. These two maids remained with the Bishop until his death. Then Lady Seton-Steuart of Touch[17] and Allanton asked them both to go to her. Mrs. Morrison did so, and was at Allanton as housekeeper for many years; but Jenny said "Na Na, my leddie, you and me's best apairt"! and "my leddie" did not take her refusal in bad part, but made her promise that she would spend all her holidays at Allanton, which she did. This Lady Seton-Steuart was grandmother of Sir Alan, the present Baronet, and was very imperious and high-tempered. She was heiress of Touch and Allanton, Seton of Touch, Steuart of Allanton. She married Sir Reginald MacDonald of Staffa, a spendthrift. When her son, Sir Henry, succeeded to the estates on her death he wished to take his father's

12 Completed 1812, on land donated by the Burgh of Stirling, to provide a public place for military parades.

13 The Valley Cemetery was laid out in 1850 through the generosity of William Drummond (1793-1868) of the Drummond Tract Depot.

14 The Penal Laws which prohibited episcopacy were repealed in 1792 and the Chapel was built in 1795.

15 Reverend Dr George Gleig born 12.5.1753, died 1840. Studied King's College, Aberdeen. Pastor at Crail/Pittenweem; appointed to Stirling 1787. Involved in negotiations for repeal of Penal Laws, 1792.

16 Upper Bridge Street in Stirling was built between 1780-1820 to accommodate the richer merchant and professional classes. Bishop Gleig's house was built to his specification.

17 An architect's model of Touch House c1740, before it was modernised, and the portrait of Prince Charles Edward Stuart by Cosmo Alexander, was gifted by Sir Alan Seton-Stewart of Touch to the Stirling Smith Art Gallery and Museum in 1918.

name of MacDonald but found he could not, or he would have had to forfeit Allanton. Sir Henry and his brother Archie were often at the bishop's house. They were both fair, and Jenny said Miss Fulton used to call Sir Henry her "White Sheep."

BISHOP GLEIG - FLORA, HIS DOG

The Bishop was very popular, and was asked to all the dinner parties. He had a great idea of his own dignity, and once when dining at Livilands, my grandfather asked the new parish minister of St. Ninians, being a stranger, to ask grace; and after dinner said "will you return thanks Bishop?" He was answered by a gruff "I play second fiddle to no man!" The Bishop had a dog called Flora, much loved by Jenny. She used to hold its forepaws, and sing to it

"It's neither Rover Cameron nor Rover MacAree.
There's no a dug in a' the toon that can compare wi thee.
An' its hey, Flora! ho, Flora! bonnie Flora Gleig!"

Flora Gleig died, and her little body was carried out to Touch and buried there.

BISHOP GLEIG. OLD EPISCOPAL CHAPEL

One of the housemaids at Touch was going to be married, and the Bishop performed the ceremony in the drawing room. Very much amused was he, when at the close of it, little Archie Seton-Steuart (Sir Allan's father) ran up to him, and said earnestly "Oh Bishop, marry me to so and so", naming another housemaid. (Dear Isobel and Leslie, you will think Auntie is writing a lot of twaddle, but I am just writing, as I recall them, all sorts of odds and ends, about your dear Grannie and her friends, that you may know as much about these faraway days as possible.)

The grandfather of John Page, Church Officer in our church now, held the same office in the old original chapel, and an old woman called Sibbie (could her name have been Sybil?) was pew opener. The Bishop was rather deaf, and when he found he had forgotten his snuff box, he used to lean over the pulpit and say in a loud whisper "Shibbie, Shibbie, get my snuff box." And Sibbie used to come back from the vestry mysteriously hiding it under her shawl and would furtively hand it to the Bishop, as if the whole congregation had not heard the whisper.

THE COLDOCH LADIES AND THE OFFERTORY

There was no other Episcopal Church for miles and people came from great distances to the services.[18] The families came from Dunmore, Leckie, Coldoch, Murrayshall, Gargunnock etc., etc., and after the service there were many friendly chats and invitations given and received. The ancient brass tray on which the alms bags are now received by the clergymen, then stood on a three legged stool in the church porch and the County gentlemen took in turns to stand by it. Our genial grandfather, greatly liked when his turn came, and had a word and smile for everyone. The three ladies from Coldoch, relatives of his own, Miss Anne, Miss Kate, Miss Clemmie, were very parsimonious. Miss Kate was gliding past "the plate" one Sunday, with a smile and curtsey to my grandfather without putting anything in, when my grandfather shouted out "Come back, Kate my woman, put something in, no curtseying for me!" They were exceedingly shabby in their dress and once when they were going down the Livilands Avenue and my grandfather was standing at the ever open door, they were astonished that he made no sign of recognition. "John Murray, do you not know us?" "Preserve us all", said he mischievously, "did I not think it was three beggar wives coming down the avenue!" And they were not a bit put out by his joke! Somehow people never could be very angry with merry-hearted John Murray. Then he was so handsome, and beauty goes a long way in winning hearts.

Christmas Day used not to be kept in Scotland except by Roman Catholics and Episcopalians,[19] and I have heard Mother say, that going to church on Christmas Day with prayer books in their hands, they would be asked "why are you going to the chapel today?" Times are changed since then.

MRS ALEXANDER MURRAY AND MENIE MACKENZIE

Mrs Alexander Murray, (Old Isobel) lived in a house at the foot of King Street, known as Dr Gillespie's Land. The windows faced King Street, but her door was in Murray Place. I remember this house being taken down, and on the site Peter Drummond, the seedsman, built his Tract Depot.[20] It in turn has been removed, and the British Linen Bank is now there. Mother always spoke lovingly of Grandmama. She was a very stately old lady, always wore grey silk, and walked with a staff. She dined once a week with our grandparents. Aunt Duthie said she owed much to the religious teaching she got from her grandmother. She was a staunch Episcopalian as all the Wordies were. They were also excellent Jacobites, and one John Wordie of Cambusbarron met Prince Charlie and his friends on their way from spending the night at Touch, and gave them wine and cake. The Wordie crest and motto are now on some of our old China bowls.[21]

18   Stirling was a centre of worship in this way for other denominations. The Reverend Ebenezer Erskine (1680-1754) leader of the Secession Church attracted huge congregations, with members travelling from all over central Scotland to hear his preaching.

19   Present giving took place on Handsel Monday, the first Monday after the New Year. When the Calendar was reformed in 1752, 11 days were removed from the month of September. Many Scots resented this change, and added on the 11 lost days to the beginning of the year, so Handsel Monday became the first Monday after 12 January. This tradition remained for over a century, and the Stirling Sons of the Rock are almost the only individuals who still celebrate Auld Handsel Monday in the 1990s.

My great grandmother's servant was Menie Sym. Menie is the Scotch diminutive for Marion. She married a man called Mackenzie and had three children, Mary, who died, called after Aunt Duthie; Isabella Murray, called after mother; and Daniel.

Isabella became our parents' servant, and I shall tell her history later. Danny was a wild boy, and behaved badly in Bryce the Booksellers shop in Glasgow where he had been placed by my father. This offence was overlooked, and he went to sea. He fell overboard, and his ship mates were horrified to see him snapt up by a shark. Poor Menie never knew this, however; she only heard he was drowned. Menie lived in a red tiled house in Murray Place,[22] which I remember seeing taken down in 1860, just round the corner from where her old mistress had lived. After her husband's death, she became a ladies' nurse, and was with our Mother when we were born. We often feel sorry we have no sketches of these picturesque old houses, such as Menie's.

For some time before Bishop Gleig died, he was a little forgetful and childish. He was always imagining it was time for family prayers, and rang his bell to summon the household. Sometimes if Miss Fulton was busy, or a little tired of the prayers, she would say "Oh Jenny, go you to the Bishop." And Jenny would go, and say "Indeed, Bishop, we canna come the noo, we're a' thrang!" And the good man would shake his head and say "Oh Jenny, Jenny, you wee Presbyterian body!" And let her go, with this mild rebuke, only to forget, poor old man, in the course of a short time, and ring the bell, with the same result. When he died, Miss Fulton gave Jenny one of the two hairbrushes he always used, and Jenny set great store by it, and never used any other brush for her hair. Once, as a great favour, she let Mr Wilson our clergyman see it. Brushes must have been much better made then, than they are now.

20 The Drummond Tract Depot (later the Stirling Tract Enterprise) was established by Peter Drummond in 1848 to issue tracts on Sabbatarian, religious and temperance matters. It became one of the largest Christian publishing houses in Britain and exported world wide. It closed in 1980

21 Much crested porcelain for Scottish families was ordered and imported from China in the 18th century. The first Scottish delft works were set up in 1748, and the Murrays of Polmaise had a dinner service with their family crest made in Glasgow Delftfield Pottery. Pieces from it are in the collections of Glasgow Museums.

22 Murray Place opened in 1843 as a new street, named after William Murray of Polmaise. It soon became the site of substantial shops and dwelling houses, and the older houses were demolished.

Miss Ann Stirling, sister of the Laird of Garden, and great aunt of Mr James Stirling, the present Laird, lived in the house next to Melville Place. When the children went in to see her, she used to regale them with stewed prunes. Another family, the Mouatts, lived near. One of them, Frank, was very vain of his appearance, "Don't you think me handsome, Jenny?" said he to Jenny McNab. "Deed, sir," said she dryly "ye would thole amends!" The Miss Colquhouns lived in the house next to Melville Place, number 4.[23] They had a servant, Kitty, who according to the custom then, when servants stayed long in their places, went by the name of Kitty Colquhoun. One summer, a wasps nest (Scottish bike) on a gooseberry bush in the Miss Colquhouns' garden, caused them great annoyance. Kitty determined to put an end to it; and one day the nursery party at Melville Place were delighted by seeing Kitty with a big knife cut off with one blow the branch on which it hung, and holding it well up, rush madly round the garden. Out flew the astonished wasps! On rushed Kitty, till not a wasp was left in the "bike", which she afterwards presented in triumph to Alick, and it lay in the sideboard drawer for many a day. It was a mad proceeding, but Kitty had not a sting. She knew what she was about, for she ran against the wind.

THE KNIGHTS' SILVER CROSS

There also lay in the sideboard drawer (that sideboard, dear Isobel and Leslie, which is now at Glentirran) another relic, namely the silver cross with St Andrew on it, which is now in our corner cupboard. In digging near St Ninian's Well,[24] right opposite Melville Place, a coffin was found. In it was the skeleton of a knight, which soon crumbled away on being exposed to the air. I think Mother said his legs were crossed. If so, it probably meant that he was a crusader. But I am not sure. On his breast, was this cross with a rosette of blue and white ribbon. The ribbon after a time crumbled away. With this nameless Knight, I always associate the lines,

> *"The Knights bones are dust*
> *His sword is rust,*
> *His soul is with the saints, I trust"*

---

23 Melville Place became Melville Terrace on expansion and feuing between 1803 and 1821. No 4 is now the Terraces Hotel.

24 A single storey stone building in the Wellgreen Business Park car park houses what remains of St Ninian's Well, which was once a main source of water in Stirling at the centre of the town's washing green. It can be located by walking down the lane opposite the entrance to Melville Place House (now 3 Melville Terrace).

25 The author Elizabeth Hamilton (1758-1816). Her novel 'The Cottagers of Glenburnie' was highly acclaimed for its insights into contemporary Scottish society.

A great friend of my great grandmother's was Eliza Hamilton,[25] who lived at Ingram's Crook. While living there she wrote her celebrated work, "The Cottagers of Glenburnie." The Crook was used by the late William Murray of Polmaise (who married Miss Maxwell of Monreith) as his factor's house and the late Mr McMicking, while acting as such, lived there for many years.

LETTERS

The style of letter writing now is very different to what it was a century ago. We dash off a few lines, and do not take time for nicely turned sentences. Postage was high. Even so late as 1835, a letter from Glasgow to Edinburgh cost 7d; and from Glasgow to London 1/1d and Members of Parliament and peers, were constantly asked to "frank" letters as it was called. By writing their names outside the letter, (envelopes there were none) the letter went free.

SCHOOL DAYS AND PATIE MACDOUGALL

Mother was a very delicate child, and for two years was never out of the Melville Place nursery. I have the little old chair, on which she sat. When she grew stronger, she went to classes at the High School with her sister and brother. Writing and Arithmetic were taught by Mr Peter Macdougall, known as Patie Macdougall, assisted by his nephew. "Patie" wrote a book on arithmetic,[26] an excellent one, of which he gave copies to Mother and Uncle Alick as prizes, with their names of the first page, exquisitely written by himself. I think a child in these days would look rather blank, if he or she, received as a prize an arithmetic book!

Bonnets were then very large:

> "Tis a charming new bonnet, set high up and poking,
> Like a pot that is set to keep chimneys from smoking",

was said of the Duchess of Oldenburg's bonnet. Aunt Duthie used to find her big bonnet very useful in school hours. Instead of doing her sums, naughty child, she would write letters on her slate to her companions, holding her head well down, so that "Patie" should not see under her bonnet, and then surreptitiously pass the slate to whoever it was written to.

But one day, "Patie" found her out, and was proceeding to make an example of her, when up got the high spirited child, and ran out of the school,[27] and

26 *The Schoolmaster's Manual, being a course of practical arithmetic, more especially designed for the use of scholars attending the Mathematical Academy at Stirling,* 1806. For further information on Peter Macdougall (1777-1851) see *Old Faces, Old Places and Old Stories of Stirling* by William Drysdale (2 vols) 1898.

27 The High School, rebuilt in 1854-6, was situated in Spittal Street/Academy Road and is now the Stirling Highland Hotel. The Back Walk adjoins Academy Road.

down the Back Walk. After her in hot haste rushed Patie shouting "Come back, you randy, Mary Murray." Whether Mary Murray returned that day or not I do not know, but no doubt she would have to apologise when she did go back.

BOGLE HA'

They had lessons in French from a Frenchman who lived in Bothwell's House.[28] That is the house with the turret staircase at the top of St John's Street, near the East Church. In it lived Queen Mary's Earl of Bothwell. After he left it, it was uninhabited for some time, because of his evil fame. Then when the plague raged in Stirling, everyone in "Bogle Ha'", as it was called, died, and again for a period it was empty.

SPINNING

Sometimes between the hours of their classes, the children used to go to the house of an old woman, who was always busy at her spinning. There dear Mother got her first lesson in spinning; and after many long years, when she herself possessed a spinning wheel, spinning became her great delight. And how beautifully she spun, such straight, even threads! "Mam" said old Finlayson the weaver at Torbrex, admiringly passing a thread through his fingers, "it wad mak flannel, be's wincey." But into wincey it was made, purple and black stripe, and we all wore petticoats of it. I wear now a black and white striped petticoat, spun by her dear hands.

WATERLOO

Mother quite remembered hearing the Castle guns fire when news of the victory at Waterloo arrived. In these days, when the fear of the French invasion was strong, nurses would frighten naughty children by saying they would be given to "Boney."[29] Even when I was a small child, Mother would say when I cried, "O what a face! enough to frighten the French." Many were the terrible things Alick vowed he would do to the French if they came. The threatened invasion was a very real fear in those warlike times.

JANET BUCHANAN

For two years, Janet Buchanan of Dowanhill, afterwards Mrs. Pollock-Morris of Craig, lived with my grandparents. She was an only daughter and as it seems odd that her father and mother should have parted with her, but perhaps they thought she was better to be with other little girls, than to be alone with her brothers. There was no money arrangement on either side,

---

28   Now re-identified as the house of Bruce of Auchenbowie, it dates from about 1520.

29   Fear of invasion by Napoleon Bonaparte ("Boney") was brought to an end by the British victory at Waterloo, June 1815.

both families being well-off, it was only a question of friendship, the Dowanhill Buchanans being kinsfolk of my grandmother's.

DOWANHILL "NODDY"

Sometimes the nursery party with Jenny in attendance went to pay a visit at Dowanhill. They went by coach, and canal, and were met in Glasgow by the Dowanhill carriage, which was a covered conveyance of the sort then known as a "noddy", now extinct. I remember seeing one in early days at St. Vincent Street, Glasgow, probably among the last of its kind. It looked like a cab but the door was behind, as you now see in wagonettes.

SERVANTS

Servants in these days, were very different to what they are now. I do not mean that they are not as good and faithful servants now as then, still it is an age of change, and all classes of society seem to crave variety and excitement. Servants, like everyone else, are "advanced" now in their views; they dress more gaily, speak better, indeed the good old "Scots" tongue is never used by them now in addressing their mistress, only among themselves. They expect more liberty and get it too, and also very much higher wages. But, on the other hand, as mother used to remark, we expect much more of our servants in the way of dress, speech, and refinement than they did then. Cooks of these days always wore a petticoat and print short gown. Even in our own childhood at Calder Park,[30] Belle, the cook, wore nothing else till she "dressed" in the evening to come up to prayers.

MANNERS AND CUSTOMS - MISS CLEMIE GRAHAM

Ladies dusted the old china in their drawing rooms and washed the teacups in the dining room; to which custom we owe it, that so many of the lovely old teacups of exquisite china, some without handles, have been preserved to us. Housekeeping then was a much more serious affair than it is now, in these days of canned meats, soups and vegetables. The yearly salting of the "mart" was a great business, for no salt beef could then be bought at a butchers. It was called the "mart" because it was at Martinmas[31] that the ox was killed and salted for winter use. The correct way, when a bit of salt meat was wanted, was to take the top most piece, never to hunt, or rather fish for a particular bit, but just to eat on as it came. I have heard old Mrs. Stirling of Garden talk of the salting of the meat as a very responsible business. The last person that I knew did it, was Miss Clemmie Graham of Coldoch, the last of the sisters there. She died aged 86 on April 2nd, 1870.

30 Calder Park, family home on the River Calder near Lochwinnoch in Renfrewshire.

31 St Martin's Day, 11 November.

Tea was a luxury seldom enjoyed by the poor. Mother remembers going with Jenny McNab to buy it at 7/6d the pound. Servants called their aprons "a brat." And mother said in the nursery, the skin that forms on boiled milk, if not stirred till cool, was called by them, children, "a brat" too, i.e. an apron on the milk. Young ladies were called by servants the "Misses." The "far room" on the Nursery floor at Livilands meaning the furthest off along the passage, when used by Mother and Aunt Duthie as their bedroom, was always called "the Misses' room." The lady of the house they spoke of as "the mistress", but not "Miss's" as in England.

COTTAGE IN KING'S PARK, PATIE'S WELL

The road we now know as Park Terrace leading to the King's Park was called by Menie Mackenzie the Witches' Road.[32] Whether this really was its name or not, I cannot say, but it is not likely that Menie would invent it. At least I know of no other name that it possessed. Along this road on fine summer days, Menie would carry Mother on her back, she being the delicate one of the party, and the others trotted by her side. She used to take them up the hill in the King's Park to where the Solitary Tree now stands, where a shepherd's cottage stood. We were all sorry when this cottage was pulled down, I forget in what year, but I know it was there in 1860, but I think it disappeared soon after that.

There was a well there, known as Patie's Well.[33] The efficacy of wells was believed in then, and Menie used to make our delicate mother drink the water of the well; indeed that she might do so, was the chief object of the pilgrimage.

The King's Park[34] then, and long after, was surrounded by an old dyke of loose undressed stone, moss and lichen-covered. So, too, was the Churchyard round the East and West churches.[35] I remember grieving when I saw both these old walls taken down, some time about 1860. They were replaced by stone coping and iron railing. Looking from this house, I often long for the picturesque old dyke.

---

32 Stirling was no great witch burning burgh, but between 1562 and 1672 women were regularly prosecuted and banished for witchcraft.

33 Peter's Well. Stirling had a number of holy wells, including St Thomas', St Ninian's and Our Lady's Well. Prosecutions took place in the 17th century for 'superstitious belief' in the power of Stirling's wells.

34 The King's Park was the hunting ground of the Stuart monarchs, and is now one of the finest Victorian suburbs in Britain. The remaining parkland was used as a horse racing course 1806-1854, traces of which can still be seen, and has accommodated a golf course since Stirling Golf Club was formed in 1869.

35 The Church of the Holy Rude was physically divided into the East and West Churches in 1656, and was not restored until 1936-1940.

The Jacobite Ladies of Murrayshall
by Owain Kirby. Smith Art Gallery and Museum

Another fancy of these times, was that whooping cough could be cured by the patient being taken into one of the disused lime kilns at Murrays Hall.[36] Mother showed me one that was supposed to possess this healing virtue. It was across the Bannock Burn at Murrays Hall, on the Sauchie side, and O the chill damp of it! I wonder if any cures were effected, but faith goes a long way towards a cure.

The old house of Leckie was one of the houses where the children visited. Mother remembered her brother Alick being there the day he was three years old, and seeing the poor little fellow taken out of bed and put upon a pint stoup in the middle of the dining room table, and told to "prophesy." (It was thought that whatever a three year old child "prophesied" on his birthday would come true! I don't know what Alick prophesied.)

The Graham-Moirs built the new house of Leckie later. They were relatives of my grandfather's. There were pleasant visits, too, to Polmaise. The laird and his lady were very popular. She was a Miss Maxwell of Monreith, and was, in her time, the queen of the county.

MURRAYS HALL

There are letters from her to my Mother when she was delicate, beginning "my dear good little girl." Many happy visits were paid to Murrays Hall. (If you look in Auntie Jean's "tree book" dear Isobel and Leslie, you will find Miss Callander's charming account of "the Jacobite ladies of Murrays Hall",[37] so I need not repeat the story here. Auntie Jenny, Auntie Lily, and Auntie Mirran (Scottish for Marion) were deservedly loved.) There in our grandfather's childhood, did he stay on a visit. And once the good ladies got a terrible fright. The child could not be found. At last, they spied him, as they thought, standing beside the Solitary Tree on the top of the steep crag. In fear they looked, but suddenly the thing took wing, and flew off! It was an eagle.

Mother said she remembered a pudding they always had at Murrays Hall. No doubt the good ladies thought it safe and wholesome for young bairns. We still call it the Murrays Hall pudding. A well buttered bowl, not a mould, was lined with rice that had been boiled in milk. It was filled with strawberry jam, covered over with rice, and then steamed for one hour. When it was turned out, if properly made, it had the appearance of a large

---

36   Possibly in use in the early 1700s, but no written record survives. Other limekilns in the area supplied lime for reclamation of the carse of Stirling.

37   Marion (d.1821), Jenny (d.1823), and Lily (d.1829) Wilson were the daughters of Jacobite lawyer William Wilson. These 'Jacobite Ladies' nightly toasted 'the King over the water' and kept alive the Jacobite songs, stories and traditions in Stirling district for as long as they lived.

snowball. And how the jam got into it was as great a puzzle to the little ones, as how the apples get into the apple dumpling was to King George III.

The ford at Bannockburn was the children's favourite place for playing. Ethel Munro kindly photographed the burn for me at the ford, where dear Mother used to wash her doll's clothes. The old house of Murrays Hall still stands; but when Mr. Campbell, your grandfather, my dears, rented it from Colonel Murray, the house was much altered, greatly to our grief. It is an ordinary farmhouse now but full of memories of the past. When Mr. Gleig, the Bishop's son, Chaplain General of the Forces, wrote his novel "Alan Breck" he called Murrays Hall in it "Cauld Hame."[38] "It was never a cauld hame to him", said the indignant old ladies. No, it was anything but a cauld hame to anyone who stayed there, and the sweet influence of the old Miss Wilsones must have had a lasting effect on the characters of their young guests.

MURRAYS HALL LADIES

The "Ladies" were staunch Jacobites and Episcopalians, and used to drive to the "Chapel" in their "noddy." Mother said, in walking to Stirling, some of the Murrays Hall ladies or their friends, would accompany them, "convoy them" is the Scotch expression, as far as the old tree, half way, known as the Seven Sisters. And the same if anyone was going from Stirling to Murrays Hall.

There was a certain Mary Love, a cotter's child at Murrays Hall, with whom mother used to play. She married, and is the mother of Shirra, the bookseller, in Port Street. Miss Callander remembers her in her childhood too, and went to see her when she was visiting us three years ago. Though the children were educated at the High School, they did not associate with any of the children. Their friends were the Campbells, your great grandfather's family, and the Birches, who lived at 5 Melville Place.

MARY ARABELLA FORBES AND MR BIRCH

Mrs Birch had a romantic story. She lived in that house which belonged to her father Mr. Forbes. She was a girl of fifteen, playing in her father's garden, wearing a pinafore. She eloped with a young officer in the Castle, Mr. John Birch, Lieutenant in the 73rd Highlanders. One morning she asked her younger sister Eliza, to go with her for a walk, which Eliza, unsuspectingly did. They walked across the old bridge of Stirling and at the other side, on the Cornton Road, found a chaise waiting and Mr. Birch. He quickly helped Mary in, and with a "Goodbye Eliza", drove rapidly off. Poor Eliza, much scared, rushed home, and announced "Mary has gone off in a chaise with

---

38 Part of the village of Kippen is known as 'Cauldhame'. Reverend Robert Gleig (1796-1888) son of Archbishop Gleig, author of several books including *The Subaltern* (1825) and *Alan Breck* (1834), served in army 1813-14, and took Holy Orders in 1830.

Mr. Birch!" Mr. and Mrs. Forbes speedily got another chaise, and pursued the runaways. They overtook them at Perth, where they were immediately married, and brought back to Stirling. I have heard Mother say, that Mary Annabella Forbes was playing in her father's garden with a pinafore on one day, and the next was a wife.

When Mrs. Birch was sixteen her first child Henrietta, afterwards Mrs. Bell was born; and soon after Mr. Birch was ordered off to India, or the West Indies, I forget which. When he and his wife arrived at Portsmouth, they found the ship was not to sail for another week, and the poor child-mother was seized with a longing desire to see her baby. Off she started from Portsmouth to London, and from London a three day's journey by coach to Stirling, got her baby and went straight off again, arriving at Portsmouth just in time to get on board the ship. When next she came to Stirling she had nine children. She and her husband and family lived at 5 Melville Place and she was the great friend of our grandmother. Naturally the children of both houses were great friends too, and constantly met. And all through Aunt Duthie's and Mother's lives, this friendship was kept up. Henrietta, Mrs. Bell, still lives and Jane Anne corresponds with her. "Thine own friend, and thy father's friend forsake not." Aunt Duthie and Henrietta Birch made what they called a Post Office, and posted letters constantly to one another. They fastened a little box on the gates of their father's houses, and there was great excitement in watching a letter being put in and then running to the gate to fetch it.

THE WRIGHTS OF BROOM

Other little friends were the Wrights of Broom. Broom is a place near the Forth lately sold by the proprietor, the Reverend Patrick Wright-Henderson of Oxford, to Mr Morris-Stirling of Gogar. It was sad to sell it, because it has been in the family for many long years. They are descended from the "Wright"[39] who pulled out the pin of the bridge, at the Battle of Stirling Bridge, and so gained the victory for the Scots. He was called "Pin Wright" after that. The Mr. Wright of our grandparents' time, lived abroad for some years, and at Florence in Italy was born one of his daughters, named Florence after her birthplace, but always known as Flo. She still lives (1894) in the house in Pitt Terrace, where her parents lived when they returned from abroad. Another daughter was called Hamilton, and became the wife of the Reverend Robert Henderson, Bishop Gleig's curate and successor. Hamilton Wright was about nine years old when she came to Stirling. Mother remembers her being held up as a model of industry to her, because she had been seen hemming pocket handkerchiefs. Mother added that she did not have a very cordial feeling to her in consequence! What child likes to have another held up as a model!

---

39 'Good John Wright' is said by the poet Blind Harry to have aided William Wallace's victory, 11 September 1297, in this way. The first born son in the Wright family thereafter was nicknamed 'Pin'. The last Pin Wright died in 1900.

Alick had a rocking horse sent to him from London by his Aunt Mackenzie. He was a very tiny child then, and when he was asked what he would call his horse, he answered "Jenny" so dear was his nurse Jenny to him. So the horse was called Grey Janet, which name it bears to this day. And you, dear Isobel and Leslie, of the third generation, enjoy riding on it still. Truly we are a fine conservative family! As Alick grew older, he had a grey pony. I think it, also, was called Grey Janet. Jenny Welsh's brother-in-law, told mother and me, on one of the last times we saw him, that often as a boy, he went to stand on the terrace to watch him mount. "And O Mrs. Wright", said old James Glen, "mony a time I envied Master Alick!" Some years ago, while we were at Park Terrace, a venerable looking, white-haired old man came to see Mother, a Mr. Blackadder from England, brother-in-law of Harvey the watchmaker here, and Sir George Harvey, president of the Royal Scottish Academy (both Harveys are dead).[40] He said he had been at school with Alick, and had dearly loved him, in spite of difference in social position, and he felt he must come and see Mother. I remember her saying after he left, "And to think Alick would have been as old as that if he had lived! I always think of Alick young."

JENNY MCNAB'S SILVER SPOONS

Dear Mother was devoted to her brother Alick. She went by the name of Tibbie in nursery days. Indeed much later; for there are letters written by Uncle Alick to her when she was visiting Aunt Duthie in England, in which he says "Jenny sends her love and duty to Miss Tibbie." It is the Scotch pet-name for Isabella. Jenny herself could not write, and Mother always wrote her letters for her. In grateful acknowledgement of this, Jenny gave her a present of six silver teaspoons, which Mother always treasured in her dressing box.

CONTENTS OF LADIES' POCKETS

Ladies then had more capacious pockets than we wear now. As well as their dress pockets, they had pockets in their petticoats, or "side pockets" as they were called, tied round their waists, under their dresses. These side pockets were made of strong white stuff, called Jean (pronounced Jane). By the way, I remember when Mary and I were at school in London, Mr. Weigall, our old drawing master, came in one day laughing, and said he had just seen in a shop in-an-out-of-the-way street, a placard in the window, with "Come and look at our stout Jane!" (The poor draper really meant this for Jean the stuff).

40 Sir George Harvey P.R.S.A (1806-1876) was a native of St Ninians near Stirling where his father was a clockmaker. Many of the sketches for his great paintings were done in Stirling, and the Stirling Smith owns 74 oil sketches, the contents of his studio, presented by his niece, Miss Nellie Harvey, in 1935. These comprise a portrait gallery of the ordinary people of Stirling in the period 1840-60. Two of Harvey's notebooks were gifted to the Smith in 1996 by William Walker.

In the capacious pockets of which I speak more things were carried than we now do, indeed, we have only room for a small pocket handkerchief. But ladies of that time always carried as well, a pocket pin-cushion, silver teaspoon, penknife, or fruit knife, a silver thimble, and sometimes a housewife with needles, thread and scissors. When we were children, Mother had all these things in her pocket except the housewife. She also carried a pencil, and a small gold vinaigrette. These were tiny gold or silver boxes, with an inner perforated lid under which lay a sponge, soaked in ammonia. I have a very old silver one, which belonged to Aunt Jane at Calder Park, with an inscription on the top, "to a friend", written just like that, no capital letter to begin with. It is no doubt very old. Mother gave me a very old silver pocket teaspoon,[41] with IC on it, belonging to some ancestress (a daughter of George Murray, my great great grandfather, married a Mr Carmichael in Edinburgh. Either she, or her daughter, embroidered the old blanket, crewel work, 1705) which I prize, but ladies no longer carry silver teaspoons in their pockets. A gold or silver pencil was also in the pocket; so you see, dear Isobel and Leslie, our grandmothers and great grandmothers went well equipped against all emergencies.

NAPERY

Sheets and tablecloths, etc., were handspun, and handwoven, and every bride carried a large supply with her to her new home. It was called in Scotland "napery" from the French word "nappe" a cloth. And the feather bed, blankets, counterpanes and napery were called the bride's "plenishin'." In our time even, it is still said among the working classes of a well provided bride, "she has had a guid plenishing." The "tocher" was the money with which the father endowed his daughter, answering to the English "dowry" or "dower." The old homespun napery was worth having. It lasted a lifetime, nay, many lifetimes, for we have the remains of the napery of many brides. On an old linen sheet which was in use till 1889, I noticed the initials MH for Mary Hutton. She must have passed it on to her daughter Jane, for on another part was JB for Jean Buchanan. Great, great, great grandmother, dear Isobel and Leslie, was this Mary Hutton, afterwards Mrs. Buchanan of Croy, so the sheet had seen five generations. This will show you how good linen was made in those days. Indeed now, in this year of grace 1894, we are still well-supplied with linen of our ancestresses; and the only time I can remember an addition made to our stock was in '84 or '85, two pairs of small linen sheets being bought, to suit the small beds in Arran, and about the same time one and a half dozen towels were got. Most of the sheets were double, but in 1887 I cut them in two.

---

41 In the 17th century and earlier people carried their own spoons for dining. This was long before the introduction of tea. St Margaret of Scotland's charity work was praised, as she fed seven orphans daily "with her own spoon."

Modern servants objected to the immense length of double sheets, and they required a large tub to be washed in, and were besides troublesome to fold and mangle. On all sheets, were several loops of tape all round. These were intended for pegs to be put in, and pegged down to the grass, because washing and bleaching were much more arduous then, than now. All the linen was laid on the grass, and well watered with a watering pot, again and again. People are in too great a hurry for all that now. The last of our servants who really bleached properly was Jenny Welsh, who left us on February 14th 1883.

Some of our old tablecloths have lovely patterns. A favourite old pattern was the "dambrod" pattern, so called because it was in squares, like a backgammon board, of which that is the Scotch name.

THE "AULD HOOSE" SHEET

We still have part of a sheet, marked in linen thread in chain stitch, the "auld hoose." This we prize, because it must have been one of the sheets belonging to the auld hoose of Gask,[42] of Lady Nairne's most touching song. And, being so specially marked, may possibly have been used by Prince Charlie. The poor dear old sheet was discovered by me, and Mother and I put it carefully aside, no longer to be used, so carefully that we forgot where it was! And shortly after her death, when I was tearing up some old linen, I found to my horror, that I was tearing up the auld hoose sheet. I remember the tears ran down my face, I was so sorry. But we saved the bit with embroidered name, also another bit, which I marked. The picture of the Auld Hoose of Gask hangs in our drawing room. It was painted by Caroline, Baroness Nairne.[43]

LAME BEGGARS

Tramps and beggars swarmed in the early days of the century. There was not the same police supervision then. Lame beggars got themselves carried from house to house. Their mode of progression was this. They were laid down by some Samaritan at a door or gate, and the servants in that house after giving the beggar a dole, picked him up and carried him to the next gate, where the same performance was gone through. Mother said she quite remembered running always to look, when the call came, "there's lame so and so at the gate, give him a lift." And out would go the maids, Peggy the cook, perhaps wiping the soap suds from her arms if it were washing day, but well pleased to have a little "crack" with the beggar, and to hear all the news of the town.

42　Gask House, Strathearn, Perthshire, was owned by the Oliphant family who were Jacobite. The piece of the Auld Hoose Sheet still survives in the Burns Tilley Monro family.

43　Caroline Oliphant (1766-1845) of Gask, Baroness Nairn was a distinguished songwriter and collector of Scottish folksongs. Her own compositions include *Charlie is My Darlin'*, *Caller Herrin*, *The Laird O'Cockpen*, *Bonnie Charlie's Noo Awa*.

Children's games, like their nursery rhymes, descend from generation to generation, and many are of great antiquity. Mother and her sisters and brother played hide-and-seek, hunt the slipper, and blind man's bluff, just as children now do. And at cards, they greatly enjoyed Old Maid, Pope Joan, and Beggar my Neighbour. Counting out, to find who should be blind man, or who should hide the handkerchief, is an ancient custom among children, and some of the rhymes are curious. The key to the exact meaning may be lost in some cases, but in some the origin is interesting. Children are highly conservative, and time honoured games are played with as much zest now as by their ancestors. Homer in the Illiad tells us of children digging holes by the sea shore, and making mimic castles of sand. Have we not all done the same thing? The "counting out" rhyme used in our grandparents' nursery was of course used in ours. It was;

> *"Onery, twoery, dickory seven,*
> *Alla boo, crack nuck, ten or eleven,*
> *Ping pang, musky dang,*
> *Tweedle um, twoodle um, twenty-one."*

The one on whom "twenty-one" came, was "out." A song in Stirling sung at this time by children was,

> *"Hey, cockie doodle, hey cockie doo,*
> *Did you see the Grand Duke, coming down the Bow"*

"Bow" was pronounced "boo" for the sake of euphony.

The Grand Duke in the song, was I think a Prussian prince who visited Stirling. Another rhyme of Mother's was,

> *"Here's a string of wild geese, how many for a penny,*
> *And they all flew over the Brig of Denny."*

The amusement to a baby being, to fold the fingers of one hand one over the other, and to open them suddenly to show how the wild geese "flew over the Brig of Denny." I have seen Granny do this over and over again for you two, my little loves, you the while watching with baby solemnity, and crowing with delight when the denouement came.

THE "BOOKIN" WASHING - OLD MANGLES

In speaking of linen, I forgot to say that there was always a huge washing about the spring cleaning time, called the "bookin washing", why so called I know not;[44] but it was the great washing and bleaching of house and table linen, used during the winter, winter not being suitable bleaching weather; and to wash, and not to bleach, was contrary to the ideas of our grandmothers.

Servants used to get up at 3 o'clock in the morning on washing days. "Thae was washings then", said Jenny Welsh to me, recalling her old big washings in St. Vincent Street days, and lamenting the degeneracy of modern servants, "wha dinna half wash", added she reflectively. After the washing, my grandmother used to go downstairs with the whisky bottle in her hand, and pour some of it over the arms of the washer women. This was to get the soap and soda out of the skin, and keep the arms from getting sore, a very kindly practice, I think, but what would teetotallers and blue ribbonites say to it.[45] No doubt the washer women got a little internally as well. The old fashioned mangles were huge, cumbersome things, the main part consisting of an immense open box, filled with large stones.[46] To sit on the top of this as it slowly moved backwards and forwards as the handle was turned, was a favourite amusement of the children; and one of Alick's threats if the dreaded "Boney" came was that he would put him into the mangle.

CHILDREN'S DRESS - PRINCE LEOPOLD IN STIRLING

Little boys of that period, when promoted to trousers, wore a tight fitting costume with many buttons. If you look at the old story book "Mrs. Murray and her Children", or the old edition we possess of "Sandford and Martin",[47] you will see the sort of dress I mean. Little girls wore short sleeves and had their necks bare; and the waists of their frocks were just under their arms.

I forgot to mention among friends of the children, the family of General Graham, Governor of Stirling Castle. The Governor lived in that part of the Castle known as the Douglas Room. The large room where the relics now are was the drawing room, the little room off it where King James murdered Lord Douglas was used as a pantry. The Douglas room was burnt in 1854,

44 'Bookin' sometimes denotes the use of the Bible when calling banns, prior to a marriage. In this instance, it may refer to the time of the annual practise of airing the books of a country house library on the lawn, in the sun, to check any mould growth or dampness.

45 "Little blue ribboners" were the children of members of the British Women's Temperance Association (BWTA) established 1876. The women wore white ribbons and their children, blue. The Smith has a small collection of B.W.T.A. White Ribbon badges.

46 The Smith Art Gallery and Museum has a huge wooden sheet press or 'box mangle' collected from 8 Park Avenue, Stirling, 1987. It was made by Thomas Bradford of Salford, a noted mangle manufacturer. Smaller items of clothing were folded inside sheets and tablecloths, wrapped round the rollers and then mangled flat by the box of stones.

47 *The History of Sandford and Merton, a work intended for the use of children* (1783) by Henry Sandford went through many editions in the 18th and 19th centuries.

but soon after restored as nearly as possible. It was while playing with the Governor's children in Queen Mary's garden, that Mother and the others saw Prince Leopold, afterwards King of the Belgians. He married in 1816, the Princess Charlotte of Wales, only child of the Prince Regent, afterwards George IV. She died in 1817, and it was in the summer following that he visited Stirling.[48] Mother was struck with his very sorrowful look; but he was exceedingly kind and shook hands with each of the children and patted Mother on the head. The sweetmeat we call "rock", a speciality in Scotland, was originally called Gibraltar rock, to celebrate the taking of that place by the British in 1704. We now have Edinburgh rock, and Stirling Castle rock, but originally it was all Gibraltar.

PROSPEROUS TRADESMEN. THE DRUMMONDS

A prosperous tradesman family in Stirling to this day is the Drummond family. A Drummond owned the nursery garden, and in the little cottage in this garden where Mr. Morrison the manager now lives, he and his wife brought up a large family, of which some went abroad I think, but William, Peter and Henry remained in Stirling as seedsmen and nursery gardeners; and James and Andrew as drapers. Drummonds Tartan Shop was where Gavin now is (1894) and though most unpretentious looking, everything was of the best. They were all fine looking men, and exceedingly respectful in manner. Andrew and James literally bowed down to the counter to their customers. I never saw such magnificent bowers, though we were only buying a yard of penny ribbon. These bows were an amusement to us in our young days, as they were to Mother in hers. Andrew was the favourite. In these days, people bargained in shops, and he was the most genial, and the most apt of the two, to lower his prices. When Jenny McNab and the children went to the shop, Jenny always tried to get him to serve her. "Noo, Mr. Andrew, what'll ye gie me that for?" "O mistress Janet, I really cannot give it lower," and so on. Peter, as well as being a seedsman, founded the Tract Depot. Drummond's Tract Depot in Stirling is known all the world over.[49]

DEATH OF MRS A MURRAY 1821

On February 7th 1821, Mrs. Alexander Murray (old Isobel) my great grandmother died, aged 84. She was buried in the Polmaise vault at St. Ninians on 11th February - "a truly good woman. The memory of the just is blessed." The gold headed stick, known as the Lanrick stick which she latterly used in walking, is in our possession.

---

48 See the Diary of Helen Graham, 1823-1826, daughter of Lieutenant-General Samuel Graham (1756-1831) of Stirling Castle. It was published under the title *Parties and Pleasures* (Edinburgh 1956) and edited by Marion Lochhead.

49 The Drummond Tract Depot operated from 1848 to 1980 and distributed religious and temperance tracts world wide. The Drummond collection can be consulted in Stirling University Library.

A noted character in Stirling was Blind Alick. His surname was Lyon, and he lived in a close, now removed, between St. John Street and Spittal Street. He wore a tall hat, and long greatcoat, and always carried in his hand a large house key, which he shook about as he went along. We have, somewhere, a likeness of Blind Alick, drawn by Mother. It is said that he was blind from his birth. He was constantly to be seen, strolling up and down the Back Walk. He had a most marvellous memory for the Bible and knew it from beginning to end, and if chapter and verse were given to him, he would repeat the text at once. Nothing would baffle him, so long as he had his key in his hand. Without it, he could not recall a verse. People tried to puzzle him, by asking him for a chapter or verse which did not exist, but he was never taken in, and would retort at once, "There are not 31 verses in that chapter." He died in 1836.[50]

LIVELANDS BOUGHT 1818

My grandfather sold Croy, and bought Livelands from the Colonel Rhynd. He got possession of it in 1818, I think, but Colonel Rhynd's widow remained there for a year after his death. Then my grandparents determined to make some alterations and additions to the house, so did not move from Melville Place. You know Livelands, dear Isobel and Leslie, where the Murray-Menzies girls now live (1894). On dear Livelands, as on many another old house, one might write "Ichabod",[51] so spoilt is it by Mr Smith of Brentham Park,[52] who bought it as a speculation, built his own large house in one field, and let the rest of the land off in feus. Very badly planned feus too, I think, for they might have been planned differently, so as not to have spoilt the beautiful avenues. But of course that is only what I think, who loved the place. He wanted money.

The house is very very old, and was at one time a monastery. It is said that when the plague raged in Stirling, that all the people whom the good monks took there to nurse, lived, hence the name Live-lands.

50 See also *Old Faces Old Place Old Stories of Stirling* by William Drysdale. First Series (1898) pp140-143. The Smith has a print of Blind Alick.

51 "The Glory is departed" - a wail of lamentation. See 1 Samuel 4:21.

52 Robert Smith Junior (1838-1901) succeeded as proprietor of Hayford Mill on the death of his father in 1859. Hayford Mill was the largest factory in Stirlingshire, and the largest tweed manufactory under one roof in Scotland. When Smith built Brentham Park in 1871, he had 1200 employees. Brentham Avenue and Crescent were erected on the Livilands Estate, and Livilands itself was demolished and replaced by Westerlands, built in 1898.

Livilands Watercolour sketch by Jane Anne Wright.
Smith Art Gallery and Museum. Throughout the journal, the author
refers to the house as LIVElands, but historically the house is Livilands

There was a very sad story about two little black, or half black, illegitimate children, a boy and girl, whom a former proprietor kept in the attics. These attics were above the Nurseries, high up in the roof. The nurseries were attics too, and had sloping roofs, but the others were higher still. They were called "The Eagle's Hole", whether a name invented by our family or not, I cannot now say, but I never heard them called by any other name. They were approached by a steep, narrow trap stair[53] of unpainted wood. Indeed there was no painted wood in that high attic at all, and they were so low, that a grown up person could barely stand upright in the middle. There these children were for two years, I believe. We children always had the idea that they were entirely imprisoned there, and I cannot rid myself of the impression that they were, but let us hope that it was not quite as bad as that. Poor little things, they had evidently tried to amuse themselves as other children do by playing at "houses." For on the low ceiling was traced with a burnt cork "Lodgings to let." One of the children died, and I don't know what became of the other, poor little ones! It was all infinitely pathetic to my child-mind; and many a time I have lain in bed in the cosy

---

53 When this stair was removed, the 17th century painted panels with the Sibyls were uncovered. They were gifted to the National Museums of Scotland in 1946.

nursery below and thought of the poor little children who had lived above, and perhaps had no one to love them, who knows! But the good God is over all. This must have been more than a hundred, or a hundred and fifty years ago, perhaps longer.

DEATH OF JEAN, MRS MURRAY 1823

On June 27 1823, Christian Jane was born. My grandmother had been delicate for a long time, but there was no anxiety felt about her, as this little baby was expected and her delicacy was put down to that. But on Sunday 3 August, Mother then not 13 years old was sitting by her, Menie McKenzie the nurse having gone down to dinner. Grandmother moved in bed, and Mother was putting the clothes over her when she saw a stream of blood on the pillow. She screamed in horror to Menie, and the maids all came running, but there was nothing to be done. She never moved or spoke. Bright pretty Jean! Like my own dear Mother, she was spared the pain of knowing she had to leave her dear ones. Mrs Birch went in at once, and did all she could for my grandfather and the poor children. Mother always spoke gratefully of her kindness at that time. Grandmother was buried in the Polmaise Vault at St Ninians, Bishop Gleig officiating; and then he returned to Melville Place and christened the poor little motherless baby Christian after Aunt MacKenzie, Grandfather's only sister, and Jane after her own mother. The old fashioned Scottish custom was followed in our Grandfather's family (as in ours) about the children's names, viz the eldest son was called after the father's father; the second after the mother's father; the third after the father. The eldest girl after the mother's mother; the second after the father's mother; the third after the mother.

There is a book of cooking recipes written by my grandmother which I now have, and which mother valued as "Mamma's." Also her wedding ring, so small that it looks like a child's. And there were two earrings, topazes, surrounded by pearls belonging to her, which your mother and I, dear Isobel and Leslie, wear as rings, and value as dear Grannie's gift.

PRINCE CHARLIE'S SNUFF BOX

Another possession of hers was Prince Charlie's snuff box, a horn mounted in silver, with a tiny spoon attached. On the horn ("mull", I think it was called), is engraved "Alexa." Who she was, we know not. This relic was given to my grandmother by a friend, before her marriage. It hangs now in our corner cupboard.

After their mother's death, the children were well cared for by Jenny McNab, and Aunt MacKenzie. But my poor grandfather had no heart to go on with the alterations at Livelands, so the old house remained as it was, and they did not move to it for some time. Another relic of my grandmother's, is a beautifully worked sampler. All little girls of that time had to make a sampler and very laborious work it must have been, on the fine canvas of those days. The object was to teach children how to mark linen. In "Jean's" sampler is the alphabet, in large and small letters; sundry ornamental flourishes; an imposing looking house; and her name "Jean Buchanan, May 13th 1793." Also TB and MH the initials of her father Thomas Buchanan and her mother, Mary Hutton. And JH and MB her grandparents, John Hutton and Margaret Buchanan. John Hutton's tortoiseshell silver mounted snuff box is in our corner cupboard. It bears his name on it, and head of King Charles I. This John Hutton was your great, great, great grandfather, my dear Isobel and Leslie.

I copy a letter written to my grandmother by Mr Buchanan of Dowanhill, after his daughter Janet had returned from Melville Place where she spent two years. With it he sent a silver salver.

"Mrs Murray, Melville Place, Stirling. My dear Madam, it affords me great satisfaction to hear from time to time of the improved state of your health. The arrival of Mrs Mackenzie will tranquillise and comfort you more and more - Janet, poor woman, retains a grateful sense of your kind attentions, during the years she was under your Roof, and protection, and in memorial of it, requests that the accompanying Waiter, may have in all time coming, a place on your Sideboard. She has been requested to write you. Whether she will venture, I know not. Should she not have nerve for it, you will I trust excuse it. Believe me, my Dear Madam, yours sincerely, Ja: Buchanan. 14th June 1823."

How appallingly formal were letters in these days even between intimate friends! How disrespectful and flippant our letter would appear to our ancestors! I do not suppose that "Janet, poor woman," did find nerve to write, at least if she did, her effort has not been preserved. And a few weeks after, my grandmother died.

MR BUCHANAN OF DOWANHILL AND MARY HUTTON

This Mr Buchanan, though he wrote so formally, no doubt had a very tender feeling for his ward, her mother Mary Hutton, having being his first love, perhaps, who knows, his only love. For years afterwards when his wife died October 21st 1842 he, then an old man, told a pathetic little tale to our own Mother. It was at Dowanhill on the funeral day, and Mother was sitting with him, while the mourners were assembling. He told her that once when he was at a funeral in the Ramshorn Church in Glasgow, and the grave was next to Mary Buchanan's, nee Hutton, he saw a skull had been dug up. "And I knew it was hers" said the old man weeping, "I knew it was hers by the bit of auburn hair." "Father", said his son John coming in at that moment, "we are ready now." And the old man rose, and went; but the tears that ran down his face were not for the wife he was following to her grave, but for the love of his youth with the auburn hair. And Mother, this Mary's grandchild, was left pondering on the strangeness of it all (Mr Buchanan died April 1844).

My grandfather's sister Christian, who lived with him till his second marriage, was born July 8th 1776, and married Captain Hugh MacKenzie, 71st Regiment, son of MacKenzie of Kincraig, Ross-shire. Her miniature is in the corner cupboard. She was tall and handsome, fair, with blue eyes, and was much loved by all her friends. The following letter was written to her when she was nearly thirteen years old. It will show the sort of letters children then wrote to one another. It is addressed to "Miss C Murray, Stirling", and is written by a little friend, Isabella Graham of Coldoch, a sister of of the three old Miss Grahams about whom I wrote before. She died young at Grahams Court, Stirling, the "town house" of the Coldoch family. It is written from C-hill, Dumfries, but the name is torn off, and is dated June 24th 1789.

"My dear Christy, I embrace the opportunity of Miss Dickson going to live at Stirling, to send you these few lines. I am sorry it will not be in my power to write a long letter, as I have so many to write, and Miss Dickson goes away sooner than she first intended. I have seen a great deal of this country since I came here, which is a very fine one. Dumfries is a neat pretty Town and a very genteel society. Willy has just come from thence, but has brought no News, so must conclude with kind compliments to your Mother, Cousin and Brother, and believe me, my Dear Christy's most Affect.- Companion, Isabella Graham."

Christian is an old fashioned Scottish name, generally in those old days pronounced Kirstin. The diminutive was Kirsty but I see Isabella has written it "Christy."

THE PENINSULAR WAR. CORUNNA[54]

Uncle Mackenzie served in all the four quarters of the globe, and was in 27 engagements. Few veterans show such a length of service, not even the Great Duke himself. Aunt Mackenzie was with him in Ireland. Her mother writes to her in 1804, at Loughrea, County Galway, Ireland. She was also with him, I think, all through the Peninsular war, at any rate the greater part of it. (She returned to Stirling in 1818.)

One of her travelling boxes was that odd one in the shape of a drum, which we now have. There is a brass plate on it with her name, and 71st Regiment. At Corunna, she and other officers' wives were in one of the transports in the bay when the French opened fire upon the shipping. Amidst great noise

---

54 The Peninsular War (1809-14) was fought by the British in the Iberian Peninsula by 'the Great Duke' of Wellington and Sir John Moore (who died at the Battle of Corunna in January 1809), as a means of weakening Napoleon's Empire.

and confusion, the ladies were sent down to the cabin and instantly a heavy shot passed through it. Aunt Mackenzie, not aware of the danger, called out, "Will nobody shut that hole and keep the wind out?" I think Mother said Uncle Mackenzie was standing near Sir John Moore, when he was shot dead.

UNCLE MACKENZIE. SOLDIER. SERVANTS

Uncle Mackenzie's servant during the Peninsula War was a Robert Murray, a man of determined courage. The 50th and 71st regiments were in the same brigade at the "coup de main" at Almarez, and upon the ladders being placed, Murray and one of the 50th, happened to be together at the foot of the ladder. Murray jocularly said, "Well, I suppose the 71st lead the way as usual," and instantly rushed up. As his head appeared above the work, a Frenchman fired, and the bullet went through Murray's bonnet. Captain Mackenzie asked him what he did with the French soldier, and he dryly answered, "I put him out of the way." Murray was shot through the lungs at the battle of Vittoria,[55] where his regiment was nearly annihilated. Uncle M went to look for him, and found him stripped, and about to be buried. He examined him, and thought he felt a sensation of life, and got him saved from interment. He was living in hospital afterwards and was servant to Uncle M in Stirling. After a time Aunt Mackenzie had to be sent home to her mother for safety. Uncle Mackenzie's last battle was Waterloo.[56] He was still on foreign service, when our grandmother died, and her own mother being then dead she was able to go to Melville Place, and finally to remove with them to Livelands. We have the remains of a diary written by Aunt Mackenzie when in Ireland with the 71st, dated 1793.[57] It has been so eaten by mice, that it is not easily deciphered. She writes of her husband as Mac, the name by which she always called him.

LETTERS FROM MISS GRANT TO JEAN BUCHANAN

A great friend of our grandmother Jean's, was Catherine Grant, daughter of Mrs Grant of Laggan[58] the authoress of "Letters from the Mountains" etc. Mrs Grant after her husband's death (he was minister of the Highland Parish of Laggan) lived with her sons and daughters at Woodend, now Gartur, and later in No. 1 or No. 2 Melville Place. From the latter place, Catherine writes charming letters to her friend Jean, then a girl at Crookston in which she makes playful allusion to a probable suitor, asks Jean to give her her

---

55 June 1813.

56 18 June 1815 - final defeat of Napoleon.

57 The 71st Regiment was in India, not Ireland in 1793. The mistake has arisen due to the poor condition of the diary.

58 Mrs Grant of Laggan (1755-1838) came to Stirling in 1801 after her husband's death and took up writing to support her 12 children. *Letters from the Mountains* was published in 1806. In 1810, having established her reputation, she left Stirling for Edinburgh.

confidence, and suggests if the event takes place, how much she would enjoy "a jaunt" to the great metropolis, with her dear Jean in the character of matron. These letters Jean has carefully preserved. In one of them Catherine writes of our grandfather and Aunt Mackenzie as follows:

"To Miss Buchanan, Jas: Buchanan Esquire, Crookston, Near Glasgow. September 23rd 1806."I spent an evening lately at a Mrs Baird's where there were a number of strangers, among the rest Mr Murray and his sister Mrs Mackenzie. You know my opinion of the former already. What a sweet woman Mrs Mackenzie is. She is a general favourite in Stirling, and though much Beloved and attended to among her County Friends, she is not the least careless of the inhabitants of her native Town."

MRS A MURRAY'S LETTER TO HER INTENDED DAUGHTER-IN-LAW

Another letter, no doubt treasured by Jean was the following from Mrs Alexander Murray congratulating her on her engagement to her son, our grandfather. It is addressed to her at Crookston Castle, spelt then Cruickstone, June 26 1807.

"My Dear Friend, My son has informed me we are soon to be nearly connected, allow me to offer you my most sincere good wishes on this occasion. May every good thing in this world prove to your mutual advantage, and in the other to come. You know of the purchase he has made, and intention of building, but as that will take some little time ere it will be executed, I hope you will have no objection to come and spend some months in my small House. You have seen it, shall say nothing as to the size, but be assured of hearty welcome from me, and shall do what is in my power to make it agreeable. You will then be on the spot to give your opinion and advice as to your own House, etc. etc. It will by no means incommode me, would not wish you to go to any other. Much Company my house won't admit, but with willing minds we shall contrive to see our Friends. Mrs Mackenzie begs to offer her affectionate regards, and would willingly comply with your and Mr and Mrs Buchanan's most kind request of visiting you soon, but an unforeseen accident prevents her. She looks forward to that pleasure ere she calls you by the name of sister. I beg to offer my kind respects to Mr Buchanan and also Mrs Buchanan, although not acquainted, but hope to have to have that pleasure soon. And believe me to be, my Dear Friend, yours with sincere affection, I Murray."

LETTER FROM AUNT MACKENZIE TO JEAN

And the "sincere affection" this pure, good Isobel then felt for the young daughter-in-law to be, increased as the years went on, and was warmly returned. Aunt Mackenzie proved a good sister, and acted a mother's part to Jean's bairns. This letter, written by her when the 71st was stationed at Weeden Barracks, Jan 15th 1819, shows her affection for Jean:-

"By this (time) John has got possession of Livilands, may you both and yours long enjoy it, it is a most comfortable residence. How often we said to one another, when I little thought you would ere be the lady of it. No doubt you must have felt a sense of pain parting with Croy; where you have acted by the advice of friends who were interested in you and in your family, one ought to look forward with confidence that all has been done for the best, and I make no doubt if you are both preserved, and blessed with health that you will find every comfort and happiness which may God of his infinite mercy grant. The great duty you have paid our dear Mother, my dear Jane, will I trust return to you a hundred fold. I never can repay you."

Alas! poor Jean never lived to become "the lady of Livelands." But she had the pleasure of making plans with her husband for improving this place before her bright life ended.

LETTER FROM MRS MURRAY OF POLMAISE TO ISABELLA MURRAY

Letter to Mother, when she was a little child, from Mrs Murray of Polmaise.

"My dear Isabella, I am very sorry to hear you are so unwell, but you are so good, so patient, and willing to take any medicine, that I hope God will soon restore you to health. I got a nice doll for you yesterday, and we are dressing her in a beautiful frock and Miss Murray is going to make a slip and Petticoat whenever she comes in. She is galloping on her poney after the dogs, and I dare say your Papa is there too. Give my love to your Mamma, and Brother, and Mary, and I am, my dear little good girl, your affectionate friend, Anne Murray."

Mother often stayed at Polmaise both as a child and as a young lady. This laird William, and his wife Anne, were greatly beloved. They had no children. She was a Maxwell of Monreith.

LETTER FROM MR BUCHANAN, CONGRATULATING HER ON HER MARRIAGE

Letter to Mrs Murray, our Grandmother, on her marriage, from her guardian, Mr Buchanan.

"Cruikstone Dec 15 1807. Since I parted from you, my dear Jean, it has always been on my mind to write you, but from various causes, some of a very trivial nature, it has been delayed. It is gratifying to me, in the choice you have made, that your lot is cast among worthy people, respectable, and respected. You know my partiality for "Birds of a good nest", and in reflecting on the weaknesses of such it is a source of satisfaction to think, that they seldom go out of the right course unless very unequally yoked. A good home, and favourable inward nature are good things, but corresponding good conduct becomes necessary to maintaining first impressions. You will wonder what this grave preface leads to. Simply to this, that Mrs Murray, your Mother-in-Law, has a high character as well as her Daughter and Son, and that your maintaining throughout with them a frank, uniform behaviour, will be a source of satisfaction to yourself and them. I have more than once mentioned to you the proverbial partiality of a Widow to her only Son. You will draw the inferences that follow, and will be rewarded by the means of being popular with the Mother. Your Mother had maxims got from old Mrs Moir, which I have heard her repeat. A young married Lady resolved that in the first six weeks she would not do, or say anything that could possibly be disagreeable to her Husband. If she succeeded it was great cause gained, and worth trying to extend it to six months. If that was found practicable, it became practicable for six years - for ever. In the married state, there is not anything so essential to happiness as uniformity of temper, and it becomes the Duty of all to watch themselves in this particular. You will, I trust, forgive so much morality. You must believe it is well meant. I hope you continue to enjoy good health. Mr Murray will no doubt take care of you, although you cannot avoid being often exhibited. Our young folks are all more or less under a cold. George was two days in bed. If in health he regretted your absence, in trouble he felt it. They will, I hope soon get well again. We intended this week for the woodcocks, but the situation of the children will prevent it. Mrs B joins me in compts and every good wish to you, Mr and Mrs Murray, and Mrs Mackenzie. Believe me with MY kind regard, MY dear Madam, yours etc etc James Buchanan."

LETTER FROM JEAN TO HER DAUGHTER ISABELLA 1822

Letter from our grandmother (Jean) to our own Mother, then a child, addressed, "Miss I W Murray, James Buchanan Esquire, Dowanhill, Glasgow. August 16th 1822.

"My dear Isabella, I wrote Mary a few days ago, and cannot help being very much surprised at her not having written me; she surely has not forgotten the injunction I gave her, or the promises she made. I hope she will be able to account for her conduct in a satisfactory way. So I will expect to hear from her, or some of the family, without delay, as I have taken it into my head that she is ill. I heard from your Papa on Wednesday, at that time they were well, and Alexander delighted with the many shows he had been seeing. I hope to hear from these again tomorrow, but I am afraid they will not be home till the middle of next week, as the Levée will not be till Monday or Tuesday. You must be preparing to come home about the end of next week. I think you have made a long enough visit, and I feel very dull by myself. I will write when I see your Papa, and mention what day you are to come home. It is not the least likely that I will get to Dowanhill as I cannot leave home until your Papa returns and by that time it will not be worth while.

Jenny is no worse, she is wearying very much for her bairns, and very anxious about Alexander. I heard yesterday from Aunt Mackenzie, she is perfectly well. I hope all at Dowanhill are well, and that you have been very good and very happy. I have a very melancholy story to tell you. On Monday Mrs Birch and the three Miss Forbes (Mrs Birch's sisters) went to Edinburgh all in health and spirits. On Wed: Miss Menzies had walked to Leith, and got herself wet. She was instantly seized with inflammation, and died yesterday morning. You see, my dear, how short her warning was, and how necessary for us all to be good, and prepared for Death. She had every medical advice, and many of her friends with her; her sister Mrs Campbell was also in Edinburgh and with her at her Death. She is to be brought out and buried at St Ninians on Monday.

I wish none of you to go near Newton Lodge, for I hear three of the children have got scarlet fever. The first time you and Mary are in Glasgow, you had better get a pair of dancing shoes, and tell Mrs Buchanan to be so good as to pay them, and I will send her the money if I do not see her. I will write to some of the family next week, and give the orders about your coming home. Remember me kindly to all the family, old and young. Tell Mary if I had her by the ear, I would give it a good pinch. I am, my dear Isabella, your affectionate Mother, Jane Murray."

THE STORY OF "TWO BROOMS"

"Menzies" was Miss Forbes Christian name. In Scotland, surnames are often used as girls Christian names (eg yours, my Leslie!) the sister mentioned as Mrs Campbell was a most beautiful woman. She had a disappointment, and out of pique married the first man who asked her. This Mr Campbell was a small, insignificant looking man, who went by the name of "Two Brooms" in Glasgow. He had a ship to sell, and the custom was to tie a broom to the mast head to show it was to be sold. He was so very anxious to sell his ship, that he tied up two brooms! He was madly jealous of the admiration bestowed on his beautiful wife, and when he found a crowd of admiring young men gazing at her portrait which had been painted by Graham Gilbert,[59] and was being exhibited, he ordered it to be turned to the wall. He and she are long ago dead, but their daughters, Elizabeth and Mary, old and half blind, always come to call on us when they come to Stirling, for love of our Mother. And very nice and kind it is of them to remember us in this way.

PROPOSAL OF MARRIAGE TO ALICE MACGREGOR OF BALHADIE

In 1824, my grandfather wrote the following letter to Miss McGregor of Balhadie;

---

59   John Graham-Gilbert (1794-1866) of Glasgow, was one of the foremost portrait painters of his day. The Stirling Smith has a handsome portrait of the young Georgina Smith by him. Its restoration was sponsored by Nina Cockerill in 1998.

"Livelands, Dec. 24th 1824.

My dear Madam, At a season when people are exchanging compliments, allow me to offer you my best thanks for the kind attention which you have shown to my young folks, to beg your Mother's acceptance of a Hare. Could I hope to prevail with you to accept an offering of another kind, how happy I should be, for I begin to suspect that you already posses that, without which the gift I would proffer would be worthless indeed. May I beg you to try if you can read my riddle, and with every good wish to Mrs Macgregor and yourself, believe me to be; Dear Madam, yours most sincerely, John Murray."

To this the following answer was returned;

"Stirling 29th Dec. 1824

Dear Sir, I will not pretend to say I did not understand your Riddle as you please to call it, but immediately showed it to my Mother, as I take no step of importance without consulting her, and she wishes for a little time to consider it, at least till we return from Edinburgh. I am sorry, Dear Sir, to keep you so long in suspense, but be assured you shall know as soon as I do myself. I must acquiesce in whatever her decision is, as without her approbation I could not be happy, being convinced she will not oppose what she thinks will be for my happiness. Believe me, Dear Sir, yours very sincerely, Anne Macgregor."

PRINCE CHARLIE AT BALHADIE. A LOYAL MAID SERVANT

The Macgregors of Balhadie were staunch Jacobites. Their "townhouse" in Dunblane still stands, and in it they entertained Prince Charlie.[60] The Duke of Cumberland and his troops passed the house, and a maid servant, not to be out done in loyalty to the Stuarts, snatched up a certain bedroom utensil, and hastily emptied its contents out of the window in the gable overlooking the road. It is said it just missed his Royal Highness's head! All honour to that loyal maid! I only wish I knew her name.

The Duke of Cumberland, was called William, and the dear old fashioned plant "Sweet William" was called after him (No, it got its name ages before from a Saint William, English Saint). I used to grieve over this as a child in the Livelands garden where it grew in all shades from pink to deepest crimson. In later days, when the primrose was chosen as Disraeli's badge,[61] there was some talk of reviving the Sweet William as Gladstone's, but it fell through, the flower being stiff, and not easily lending itself to decoration.

---

60 Jane Anne Wright's watercolour sketch of the house is in the collections of the Stirling Smith.

61 Supporters of Disraeli (1804-1881) formed themselves into the Primrose League, and wore enamel primrose badges. The Smith has good examples in its collection.

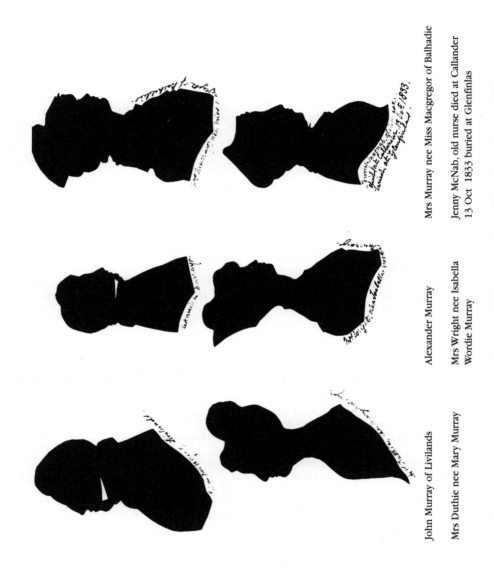

Mrs Murray nee Miss Macgregor of Balhadie

Jenny McNab, old nurse died at Callander
13 Oct 1833 buried at Glenfinlas

Alexander Murray

Mrs Wright nee Isabella
Wordie Murray

John Murray of Livilands

Mrs Duthie nee Mary Murray

Family Silhouettes

The Clan Macgregor was under a ban, the very name proscribed. They called themselves Drummond till happier days came. Among the many interesting Jacobite letters we possess, you will often find the name Drummond for Macgregor.

THE MACGREGORS OF BALHADIE

Anne's father Alexander Macgregor, was born in France, Oct. 7th 1758. He was the only child of William Macgregor or Drummond and his wife Janet Oliphant of Gask. This Alexander married his first cousin Mary Macgregor or Drummond, and had a large family, all of whom died young and unmarried, except Anne, who became our step grandmother, and Donald her brother. He was half witted and died in January 1855, the last of the Balhadie race and chief of the Macgregors. So do powerful families come to an end, and others rise up and take their place. There is a beautiful likeness in oils of Mrs Macgregor of Balhadie, Anne's mother, now in the possession of the Duthies at Row. I used to call it the "pretty lady", and stand admiring it in the Livilands drawing room long ago. The expression of her face, so sweet and pure, was a feast of delight to me then. How I loved her! It was so comfortable to feel her sweet eyes following me about the room, and she was always smiling! Mother said she was very handsome and graceful, pure and good, and dearly loved by her daughter. She had a charming sister, Margaret Drummond who lived with her, and whose most interesting diary we possess.

MARRIAGE OF JOHN MURRAY AND ANNE MACGREGOR 1826

When the Macgregors resumed their name, she still kept to that of Drummond. These two excellent sisters with young Anne lived in Bridge Street near Bishops Gleig's House, and latterly in Allan Park. Needless to say, like all Jacobites, they were Episcopalians. On September 5th 1826, my grandfather married Anne Macgregor. No doubt it must have been a trial to Mother and Aunt Duthie who were old enough to feel it deeply, but she proved one of the best of stepmothers, devoted to her husband and his family, especially to the little Jane, who did not, till she was seven years old, know that she was not her own mother. The marriage was a happy one, and Anne was a truly good religious woman. Aunt Eliza at Calder Park always spoke of her with the greatest affection and admiration of her character. The silhouettes that we have of her represent her as a stately, handsome woman, but she has not the delicate beauty of feature, or the bewitching grace of her mother. She was an excellent housekeeper, and Livelands was a house of comfort and plenty.

After the marriage, Aunt Mackenzie, whose home now was to be Melville Place was on her way to Livilands to put some finishing touches there before the arrival of the bride, when she saw the carriage with her brother and his wife in it, coming before they were expected. Off she set as fast as she could run to reach Livilands before them, so as to welcome them. She was not strong at the time, and the hurried run was too much for her, and laid the foundation of bad health.

SERVANTS AND THE NEW MISTRESS OF LIVELANDS

Jenny McNab, the old nurse, and the new lady, did not care much for one another. It was natural on both sides. Jenny clung to her bairns, and the bairns clung to her and preferred being in the cosy nursery in the evenings, where they amused themselves, and ate apples (the apple room at Livilands was conveniently near the nursery!) to being in the drawing room with the rather stately and exceedingly "proper" stepmother. She, poor woman, felt a little jealous of Jenny, could it be wondered at? But they were both excellent woman, and pulled along wonderfully well. But as is usual in the case of a stepmother, she had to reform many things, among others, the children's pocket money. Mother used to get hers from any surplus from the dairy; Duthie, I think, from the poultry. Sometimes, Mother said, she had a large sum, and Grandmamma thought it far too much, and that their father was too indulgent to them. So it was altered. But these little things were trying to the children, and much resented for them by all the old servants.

PEGGY AND THE POTATO

They too, on their own account did not like to be interfered with. One day at dinner Mrs Murray remarked that the potatoes were not enough boiled. The servant who was waiting must have told this to Peggy Morrison (aunt of Margaret McArthur), the cook. For, suddenly, the dining-room door burst open, and in rushed the irate Peggy in her petticoat print and short gown, then the ordinary dress of cooks, holding in her hand a large potato in its skin. "Dae ye ca' that no biled", said she, crushing the mealy potato in her hand under the nose of her startled mistress, and then turned and fled to the kitchen. This was an immense amusement to our grandfather and the children, but not to the step-mother. But all these little rubs were got over, and Peggy stayed on for years.

MARY MURRAY'S MARRIAGE TO MR A DUTHIE

The first change in the home circle at Livilands was the marriage of Mary the eldest child, to the Rev. Archibald Hamilton Duthie on January 9th 1828. The bride was very young, only 19 a few days before, and concerning this, old Miss Lily Wilsone of Murrayshall, sending her a tablecloth as her present, remarked that there was a slight difference in their ages, the figures were reversed, Mary was 19, and she was 91. Uncle Duthie was the son of Mr Duthie who owned Laurelhill (now in the possession of the Miss Speirs 1894) then called Mount Pleasant after his West Indian property (Its original name was Whitehill. He sold it to the Miss Erskines, who called it Christian's Bank after their mother. The Miss Speirs changed it again to Laurel Hill).[62]

---

62 The modern Laurelhill House in Laurelhill Business Park, is the headquarters of Forth Valley Enterprise.

The Duthie and Murray children had always been intimate. I have heard Mother tell how she and one of the daughters, Maria, as little girls at the dancing class held in the Guild Hall,[63] danced a little dance together on the closing day, to the admiration of the assembled parents and friends. It was put down in the programme as a "fancy dance by two little girls." They wore white frocks, and long black mittens. Long years after, in 1876, when Jane-Anne and Mother were visiting Jane and Mr Benson at Ringwold Rectory, they went to spend a day with "Aunt Maria" as she was always called, in her pretty house at Upper Deal. "Now, Maria", said Mother merrily, "here we are, do you remember our dance?" And up she got to begin. Up too got Aunt Maria and they "set" to one another, and curtsied and bobbed about, in happy remembrance of "auld lang syne." My dear happy old Mother!

Uncle Duthie was curate in Stirling, and so had plenty of opportunities of knowing his bride well. She was a most elegant, beautiful girl. We all remember her as an exceedingly handsome woman. I always think "gracious" is the word to apply to her. Her extreme modesty may have made her a little hard to win; it was said of her that if she saw Mr Duthie coming one road, she would speed away along another; but this was before they were engaged.

ALICK'S LETTER ABOUT HIS SISTER'S MARRIAGE

Her brother Alick, then at Glasgow College, writes a merry letter to our Mother at Livilands at this time:-

"My dear Isabella, I sit down to write to you a few lines at ten o'clock, which must be the excuse for blunders, as I shall not have time to write tomorrow. I hear by Aunt's letter to Mrs Lightbody of Mary's arrival. I would not like to be in her place on Sunday, what congratulations, shaking of hands, bowing, nodding, clattering, glabbering, laughing and what not; the Tower of Babel will be a joke in comparison; then the drinking of ginger wine at Aunt's, cracking of biscuits will close the theme. I hope you will be able to be there to see the fun, for even Sunday will not prevent it. I hope Mr D is in good health and spirits, and left all his friends well. I was very sorry to hear of Aunt's fall, but trust she is getting better. I almost dislocated my wrist the other morning in the same way, it is a proof of the benefit of having pliable joints. Thank Aunt in my name for her kind letter. I hope I shall have time to write her a long one soon. How is Max? I wish you to send me the small brass padlock, it is in my writing desk, the key is on the same ring as the key of the desk. I am going to put it on a brass collar of Spark's, which Mr A Cleland gave me. Spark begs his compliments to Jane for the attention she has shown in asking for him so often. She will be loaded with napkins now, I think; such a beautiful one Mr Harrow has sent her. I forgot to mention in

---

63   The popular name for Cowane's Hospital, St John Street, Stirling.

my last letter my having received the ten shillings for which I thank you, and I shall always be happy to have it in my power to ————-.

Alick's letter continued.

I am a bad hand in fine speeches or palavars. It was a lucky thing the box came on Tuesday as I had put on my last shirt. Tell Jenny I want the long pair of stockings I have sent, cut in the feet, as they will not go into one of my shoes. I hope Jenny is well, and taking care of herself. Looking up the page I see "how is Max" staring me in the face, give him my love, if he is particularly fond of snow battles, he would have got his fill the other day, we had a terrible battle in College Street[64] with some of the citizens of Glasgow, where plenty of fractured skulls were going, which ended in the Police Office. It gave some employment to the Glaziers and Doctors all for the good of the trade. I am glad Papa has got the field, but he has paid severely for it. When are we to be favoured with Mr and Mrs Duthie's visit? I cannot get my tongue about that name yet! With compliments to all, I ever am, your affectionate Brother, Alex Murray."

MR BUCHANAN'S LETTER IN 1828

Mr Buchanan of Dowanhill writes thus to my grandfather on January the 17th 1828.

"I sympathise a little with you on the great change which Mary's marriage will make in your family. For she is forever withdrawn, and if once settled she will draw occasionally others after her. But this is the ordinary march of things, and what every family may expect. I trust Mary will enjoy happiness in the connection she has formed. I beg my respects to Mrs Murray and wee Jean, which is now the pith of your family."

LETTERS FROM ALICK 1829

Aunt Duthie's marriage made a great difference to our mother in the way of companionship, but she was devoted to her brother Alick and he to her. Uncle Duthie was Rector of Hartinglaigh in Kent and when he married, later they were at Minster, Sittingbourne, and then Deal. Mother paid them long visits from time to time. Alick writes to her Feb. 22 1829.

"Some of the Town Council are wanting to feu St Ninian's Green.[65] Aunt is in a terrible kick up about it as it will shut up all the view (from Melville Place). It would be a shame to deprive the inhabitants of the washing green."

---

64 Glasgow College (the University) was in High Street/College Street from its foundation in 1451, an area later considered to be rough and disease ridden, hence the move to the present site at Gilmorehill in 1870.

65 What is now Pitt Terrace was built on part of it. St Ninian's Green is now the Wellgreen Business Park, although St Ninian's Well survives.

He also writes,

"You have no chance of chess with me now, for I beat Mrs Murray (his stepmother) every night; and what is more, I won one game with Mr Henderson (Uncle Duthies successor as curate to the Bishop) who was greatly mortified at letting me win from him.

On April 5th 1829 he writes to her,

"There is a fine coach commenced running between Edinburgh and this called the Tally-ho. Mr Ramsay of Barnton is the great hand in it, he runs two stages, and Sawers, the Innkeeper and a Mr Scott in Edinburgh run the other two. It came the first night in 3 hours, and 40 minutes."

Also in the same letter,

"Miss Birch was here last week. She is going to be married to a Captain Bell of the East India Company Service, and is to go out with him very soon."

MRS BELL. JANET BUCHANAN MARRIED TO DR POLLOK

This is the Henrietta who with Aunt Duthie made a post office for their letters on the gates at Melville Place. She is still alive (1894) and corresponds with Jane-Anne, and her beautiful handwriting at the age of 85 in August 1893, puts to shame the untidy writing of the present day.

> *"I must only add*
> *my very kind love to you and*
> *your Sisters and believe me*
> *yours very affectly*
> *Henrietta Bell."*

ALICK'S LETTER 1829

Alick writes in 1829 to Mother who was in England with the Duthies

"Mr Moir of Leckie is building a new house, it is to be a very fine house." (This is the present house of Leckie, 1894). Also,

"The new bridge here (Stirling) is contracted for, a man of the name of Mathieson has got it."

Also,

"Jenny sends her love to Miss Tibbie" (Mother)

also,

"Jenny sends her love, and is very proud Isabella is so good a traveller, and she is quite ready to take a trip to France with her, if she will only send word in time, as she takes so long a time to pack"!

JANET BUCHANAN MARRIES DR POLLOK

On the 28th of August 1829, Janet Buchanan of Dowanhill married Dr. William Pollock late Surgeon of the 53rd regiment. He was rich, so was she and somehow money goes to money. She was a very pretty plump girl, and had many admirers. She ought to have married Mr Smith of Deanston,[66] but threw him over for handsome Doctor Pollock, a haughty, overbearing man, who imagined he could rule in Scotland, as he had done in India over those who were under him. He was quite a good character and another wife might have drawn out his good qualities.

MRS POLLOK. AFTERWARDS MRS POLLOK-MORRIS

But Janet was painfully shy and reserved, and her dear kind heart (how well I knew it in after years!) was hidden under a cold exterior. But she was not really cold, she loved intensely, even to pain. But her life was far from happy. My father and aunts were great friends of the Dowanhill family. Aunt Eliza and Janet Buchanan attended the same classes in Glasgow. And after the marriage of the latter, my father and Aunt Eliza went to pay her a visit at Cunninghamhead in Ayrshire where the Polloks were then living. Ellison, the oldest daughter, born June 23rd 1830 was a tiny infant of a few weeks old. Aunt Eliza said to me "Janet was so young, not yet 21, she had her baby on her knee, but your Papa and I were so sad when we came away. She had always had a great liking for him, and he for her; and as we left the house he said to me "the heart's crushed out of Janet already!" And I saw it myself, my dear", said dear Aunt Eliza weeping, "and O my dear, what else could be expected, that is a sin that I always think is punished in this world (she meant jilting anyone) and poor dear Janet has had her punishment."

MRS POLLOK-MORRIS

In time Doctor Pollok succeeded an old cousin in the estate of Craig in Ayrshire, and took her name of Morris in addition to his own. But I think that in the long years that followed, her father, had he lived might often had said "Janet, poor woman", as he did in writing of her to our grandmother Jean in 1823. Once in 1880 when Mrs Pollock-Morris was telling me the story of her sorrowful life, I told her my father's remark about her in 1830. "Did he say that?", she said, tears running down her sweet old face, "and O my dear, it was true, the heart was crushed out of me." O me! The pity of it all!

How very different Mother's and Aunt Duthie's lives were! Cares they had,

---

66 James Smith of Deanston (1789-1850), agricultural improver and industrialist, was one of the great men
    of science in the first half of the 19th century. The Smith has a portrait of him.

and little money, but there was always Love, and that is the greatest thing in the world. Mother paid long visits to her cousin Janet. I shall have much more to tell of her, when it comes to the story of my own life, for she was very dear to me, and Mary and I were, as she often said, like her own children. When you were at Craig, dear Isobel, a six month old baby, Mrs Morris, stroking your head fondly, said, "She is like another grandchild to me!" Dear Mother was a true friend to her, and was the means of getting old Mr and Mrs Buchanan, her parents, to come and see her when she was in great sorrow at the death of her little girl Janet. Doctor Pollock quarrelled with the parents and brothers, and they could not meet. Indeed, her only chance of meeting her brothers, was in our parent's house in Glasgow.

LETTERS FROM ALICK TO HIS SISTER ISABELLA IN ENGLAND 1829

Aunt Duthie's eldest child, John James, born Nov. 11 1828, died in 1829. Mother went after his death to stay with her. Alick writes from Livilands,

"Sept. 23rd 1829, My dear Isabella it was settled yesterday that the box was not to go till the end of the week, however, last night I was told it was to go this day, which has obliged me to rise at the early hour of seven on a cold frosty morning to write to your ladyship. I am sure you will be happy to see Janet (Mrs Pollok on her wedding trip to London, they drove all the way in their own carriage), who was to be in London by the 22nd. I think it will help to keep up Mary's spirits, for poor Jack will make a terrible blank. I wish I was with you to see all the fine things in London. You are very lucky indeed to get such an opportunity, since having a carriage is such an advantage. Be sure if you can, to see the Colosseum or panorama of London. We will be very lonely without you here this winter, as Mary says she will not let you leave her, but we must hope to see you all next year some time or other. There is nothing new going on here. The new bridge is to be commenced next year, as it will take all the winter to collect materials. Papa is to begin digging a well next week, it is to be about the stack yard (at Braehead farm). I hope he will succeed. They are making a fine row in the town just now about the election of magistrates; it is thought old Provost Anderson will be made Provost, and if so, will die before the next election as he is very frail. I am sure I do not know what to tell you, and as Mrs Murray is writing, she will of course ransack her brain for some news, but I can do nothing till I get my breakfast as I am very hungry. If they had given me proper warning, I would have written you a splendid epistle, but I think I have a very good excuse. Jenny sends you and Mary her kind wishes, etc, etc, etc, accompanied by a bag of Rose leaves, which are dried by a new way she has found out, but which she keeps secret. She also sends a piece of the gown Janet (Mrs Pollok) gave her, which she is very proud of. If you were here, you would get such feasts on Pears. We have a very fine crop, both of these and Apples, and Jane and I have fine desserts after dinner. Give my love to Mary and to Mr Duthie, and burn this letter. I ever am, your affectionate Brother, Alexander Murray."

The letter was not burnt. With all the others, it was kept by Mother; she dearly loved her only brother; and kept, not only his merry schoolboy effusions, but the books he got as prizes, beginning with "Patie" McDougall's Arithmetic book, and going on to the prizes he took in Glasgow University.

On March 21st 1830, another little child was given to Uncle and Aunt Duthie, and christened Jane Buchanan after her mother. Aunt Duthie was very ill at the time, so was the baby, and so was the monthly nurse, and Mother had much to do, and was, as ever, an immense help and comfort, as Uncle Duthie's letters testify.

ALICK'S DEATH

In the autumn of that year, a great sorrow came to the family at Livilands, as well as to the many friends of the much-loved Alick. He had never been strong, and suffered from attacks of asthma, but there was never any special cause of anxiety about him. On August 23rd 1830, our Mother and Alick went to Dowanhill to pay a visit to the Buchanans; from there to Fairlie House, Ayrshire, where Doctor and Mrs Pollok then lived. It was before Dr Pollok's succeeded to Craig on Miss Morris' death. At Fairlie, Alick became ill, and so severely ill that on Sept. 29th his father went to see him, taking with him Doctor Macansh. Mother nursed him devotedly night and day, and great were his sufferings from want of breath. On Oct. 1st, Jenny Macnab went to Fairlie to help to nurse him, and everything that could be done was done by the devoted sister and faithful old nurse. It was thought best to take him home, so the three started for Glasgow, where they were met by Tom Buchanan (one of the sons of Dowanhill) on horseback. He asked Alick whether he would go straight on to Livilands, or go to Dowanhill. No doubt poor Alick was already worn out from the long journey, (there were no railways in those days), so he said "to Dowanhill." And there on the afternoon of Thursday the 21st of Oct. at quarter past three, he died.

ALICK'S FUNERAL

Next day, his poor father and Uncle Mackenzie took his body in a hearse to Livelands. The hearse entered Livilands by the old avenue, and half way upturned in to what was already made of the new one, by a white gate on the right, that new avenue of which Alick had so merrily written to Mother, that he "and Papa were busy planning the new avenue." (My grandfather had no heart to finish it after that, and it was left untouched till just before Mother's marriage.) On Monday the 25th at 2 o'clock, he was laid in his coffin, 20 people being present. In Scotland this is called the "chesting", and the clergyman is always present, and holds a little service. Then the body is reverently lifted into the coffin by the relations, a kindly tender custom that I should be sorry to see discontinued. On Tuesday the 26th, Alick was laid to rest among his ancestors in the Polmaise Vault at St Ninian's, amidst much mourning for he was universally beloved.

Weaver's Row St Ninians and St Ninians Church, the burial place of the Murrays and Wordies. Now part of Stirling. Watercolour sketches by Jane Anne Wright. Smith Art Gallery and Museum.

He was very clever, and so handsome that people used to turn to look at him in the streets of Glasgow. Had he lived he was to have control of the mercantile house of Dennistoun, Buchanan and Co., of which Mr Buchanan of Dowanhill was a partner. While attending the classes at Glasgow College, he boarded with one of the nieces of the Murrayshall ladies, Miss Margaret Wilsone, who from her odd temper, could not live with her sisters Miss Lily and Miss Janet of Graham's Court, Stirling.

When mother was paying a visit to the John Buchanans, 10 Moray Place, Edinburgh, she showed Jane Anne in a cabinet in the drawing room, a small glass lantern which had held a night light when her brother Alick lay dying at Dowanhill. Alick's death was not the only sorrow that year, for not long before, on June the 13th, the good faithful Aunt Mackenzie breathed her last at Melville Place. And so the home circle at Livilands was sadly changed, Mary married in England, Isabella often with her, or paying long visits to her cousin Janet, or the Buchanans of Dowanhill, and Alick "away", as we Scots pathetically say of our dead. I like the expression. "Dead" is so sorrowful. "Away" suggests a long journey, but a reunion. "Aye, he's awa', and bye wi' it a', is what I have often heard from poor people. "Bye wi troubles", they mean.

I do not know of anything special that happened till two years after, when the Rev. Robert Henderson proposed to our Mother and was refused by her. She was then 22. He was of good family, and an exceedingly good, gentle, conscientious man and most sincerely attached to her. Her father made great fun of "all the ministers coming after my daughters"!

MR HENDERSON'S LETTERS 1832

Mr Henderson's letter to my mother was so good and honourable, that I copy them.

"Queen Street, 28 Nov. 1832. I scarcely know how to address you dear Miss Murray, and feel afraid that you will look upon this letter as abrupt, as it will be very unexpected by you. The lack, however, of other opportunities and my own diffidence, induces me to take this mode of telling you of my attachment and entreating you as I know your frank and kind nature will prompt you to do, to tell me whether or no I have any chance. I have indeed many fears, as I know not in what light you will regard me, or whether you have a preference elsewhere; and my fears are the stronger in proportion as I the more ardently desire a favourable answer from you. All I ask of you is, to say that you will give me an opportunity of waiting personally upon you, at any time and place you may appoint. I will frankly say that I have but a small, though I trust you will find it a sufficient independency to offer you, and in the event of having the happiness of being accepted by you, it would be the delight of my life to study yours. I am sure you will keep my secret, and give me an answer which will end suspense, or allow me the opportunity of personally explaining myself. Whatever the answer will be, I shall ever remain, most truly yours Robt. Henderson."

MR HENDERSON REFUSED

Mother was at Livelands at the time and did not keep the good man long in suspense. In answer to her letter he wrote,

"Stirling, Monday, Dec. 3rd. Dear Miss Murray, I received your letter, for the frankness and decision of which, as it at once informed me that no hope was to be entertained, I thank you. I called on Mrs Murray, and entreated her to make my apology to you for the abruptness of my letter. I have since thought I should have done it to yourself, and as I could not do it personally, I beg you to pardon the trouble of this letter. Now I perceive that my letter must have appeared unusual and abrupt. What I have to say is, that it was written under a feeling of impulse, after I had seen you that day, which did not admit of consideration, a feeling (which I had often entertained during your absence from Stirling) of regret I had not hitherto had the opportunity or confidence to make myself more known to you, and also as I had heard that you were again to be away from Stirling. I wished to have expressed this to Mrs Murray to tell you, but I am not sure that in the agitation of the moment I did it fully. This will account to you for the seeming abruptness of my letter. I shall be proud of your friendly regard, I shall rejoice to hear of every happiness befalling you, and I trust that what has happened will prove no interruption to our occasional and friendly meeting in ordinary society. I remain, dear Miss Murray, sincerely yours, R Henderson."

Good, excellent, patient man, I cannot imagine that at any period of your life you ever said, did, or wrote an "abrupt" thing. Mother told us that the very day that she refused him they met at a dinner party, and he was told by the host or hostess to take Miss Murray into dinner. But he was a perfect gentleman, moreover he loved her, so he treated her that evening as if nothing had happened. But he must have suffered, O poor man, he must have suffered. And there the matter ended. But love dies hard, if indeed it ever dies. He did what many men have done in similar circumstances, married one as unlike our refined, modest, aristocratic-looking mother as possible.

HIS MARRIAGE TO MISS WRIGHT OF BROOM 1834

There could not have been a greater contrast than between her and Hamilton Wright of Broom whom he married Sept. 16th 1834, but though he must of found her excitable manner, and erratic ways trying, he made no sign, like the loyal, true gentleman he was. They lived in 16 Allan Park where their youngest son George still lives (1894), and had four sons. Two survive, Patrick, in Holy Orders, married and living in Oxford, fellow of Wadham etc, and George who as I said lives here. The two elder sons, John and Robert, were in the army and were killed in the Indian mutiny.[67] The poor father never really got over the shock and sorrow of their death, and I do not think it was definitely known how they died. It was said one of them held on to a boat, and the cruel Sepoys struck off his hands, and so he fell into the water, and was drowned.

MR HENDERSON'S DEATH

Mr Henderson died on the 16th of Feb. 1875, and was buried in the Stirling cemetery on the 22nd. His college was St John's, Cambridge. He was 78 when he died, a handsome, fair skinned-old man, of gentle, rather sad, appearance. For some years before his death, he was childish from paralysis. "He forgets everything, poor old gentleman", said his wife, with the giggle that always accompanied her remarks, "Yes, yes, he forgets everything; but one thing he never does forget, Mrs Wright, and that is to send your girls something when they are decorating the Church; no, no, no, he never forgets that; and its quite his own thought, you know, quite his own thought, and very remarkable I am sure." And I remember Mother's face flushed when she heard this. And it was touching, the old man's thoughtfulness! Every Christmas and Easter, a servant came to the Church with a large bag of buns, a small flask of wine, and a little tumbler, "With Mr Henderson's compliments to the Miss Wrights." And we always took him something from the church, a bunch of violets or holly according to the season. Another flash of memory returned to him in 1874 when Mrs Henderson gleefully told us, "I thought I would try to rouse him by telling him of your aunt Mrs Duthie's death, I said "It's Mary Murray, you know; and Mrs Wright has gone to Florence, leaving her girls alone", and he grew quite excited and said to me, "O those poor girls of Mrs Wright's, go to them at once!" Mrs Henderson died in her son's house in Oxford, May 19th 1876.

DEATH OF JENNY MCNAB

On the 19th of July 1833, Jenny McNab left Livelands. For a long time, she had suffered from cancer in the breast, but she neither told anyone, nor asked medical advice, so afraid was she that she should be thought unfit for work, and so have to leave her dear nurslings. Mother knew she had a painful swelling, but she kept Jenny's counsel, and said nothing, being likewise afraid of losing her, for she had been mother and nurse and all to her from the time of her own mother's death. But at last poor Jenny was too ill to keep silence. Everything was done for her comfort. Grandpapa not only had the local doctor, but he sent to Edinburgh for the best doctor for that disease. But there was no help for poor Jenny. She went to Callander, and there she died, and was buried in Glenfinlas. She was a native of the Brig O'Turk. The meaning of the highland name McNab, is "son of the abbot." In May 1885, when we were all at The Mollands, a farmhouse a mile

---

67   1857-8.

from Callander, we had to pass the old kirkyard on our way from the farm to the village. Mother could not remember where Jenny was buried, but fancied it might be in the old Callander Kirkyard. When she and I walked past, she often spoke of Jenny; and one day she stepped aside, and leaning against the gate, and looking in wistfully, she said again, as she had often said before, I wonder if Jenny lies there"! So I said I would go to some of the cottages near, and find out who kept the key, and then we should hunt among the tombstones; but Mother turned away rather sadly, and said "What would be the use, dear, it isn't likely Jenny would have a tomb stone."

I had a message to the baker's shop, kept by old Miss McNab, her sister, and her niece. Miss McNab, Beatrice, was stout and portly, Mary her sister, thin, and pale; and the niece, a young Beatrice, was quite a young person of the period, and a great contrast to the pleasant, old fashioned aunt. Mother told them about her old nurse, and found her to her delight, that it was in a room in their house that Jenny had lived after she left Livelands, and there she died. "O", said the two old sisters, "are you one of the Miss Murrays of Livelands! Many a time Jenny spoke of you all!" They then told us that Jenny was no relation of theirs, though she bore the same name, that she was so beloved in the village that even the children would squabble about who should be the favoured one to run her messages; and that when she died, she was taken to Glenfinlas, and there laid among her ain folk. It was a great comfort to dear Mother to have this talk about her dear old nurse, and she promised next time she came to Callander to take with her the silhouette of Jenny McNab,[68] which they greatly desired to see. But alas! "the next time" never came, and now Mother is "away" herself!

JENNY MCNAB. MARY DOW. NIECES AND NEPHEWS

Miss McNab[69] made supplies of shortbread at regular times for the Queen, ever since she supplied the Royal household when the Queen was at Invertrossachs, and while we were at Callander she gave Jim a cake of it for his "good lady", and most excellent it was. Miss McNab is dead now, and the business is carried on by her foreman.

Jenny's successor at Livelands was Mary Dow (pronounced "doo"). She remained there for 13 years. Nothing very special occurred between the years 1833 to 1841. Mother was often in England with Aunt Duthie, who was delicate, and who never was so happy as when she had her dear sister with her. Mother was devoted to her 8 nieces and nephews. When you were born, dear Isobel, she said to me, "Now you will know what I feel for the Duthies." She was "Auntie" to them, as I am to you, and was at all times the confidant of their joys and sorrows. We have charming letters written to her

68   See the silhouette on page 38.

69   A photograph of Beatrice McNab was published in *Character Sketches of Old Callander* by James MacDonald (Callander 1938) p66.

Jane Anne Wright (1842-1922)
sister of the author with her pony and trap. Disabled by a childhood accident,
Jane Anne spent her time sketching houses and landscapes in Stirlingshire, and
a collection of 81 of her watercolours was gifted to the Stirling Smith Art Gallery
and Museum in 1932 by her brother in law J W Campbell. Her watercolours are
an important topographical, historical and artistic record of the district.

by Uncle Duthie, full of regrets for her absence, longing for her return, and
all sorts of little chit chat about the children, what a "fine young gentleman"
Willie was when he was one hour old; what his name was to be; how "Jane
was as usual tyrannised over by snubbed nosed Maggie" etc, all very
interesting to the dear Auntie to whom they were addressed.

CARD PLAYING AT EGLINTOUN CASTLE

Mother also paid many visits to her cousin, Janet Pollok-Morris in Ayrshire.
It was while visiting her, that she for the first and last time played cards for
money. She was dining at Eglintoun Castle, and after dinner cards were
proposed, and she gladly joined in the game as she would have done at
home. Then she found it was for money, she having none with her, would
gladly have drawn back, but she was not allowed to do so, and someone

paid for her. One by one, the others played themselves out, till at last only Mother and a Gentleman were playing. All the guests gathered round to watch, and laid bets, some on one and some on the other, and at last Mother gained, and to her infinite horror all the stakes were swept in to her. She refused to take it, but was told she must, and while others went off to some other amusement, she was left at the table with a whole pile of money before her. She was a very young girl, and could nearly have cried with vexation, and she had no pocket in her white muslin dress, so she tied it up in her pocket handkerchief, and registered a vow never again to be beguiled into playing for money.

ARDCHULLARIE

She once payed a pleasant visit to your great grandparents Mr and Mrs Campbell, dear Isobel and Leslie, when they were spending the summer at Ardchullarie, a farmhouse near Loch Lubnaig. Dickens "Old Curiosity Shop" had just been published,[70] and your great uncle Willie Campbell used to be heard laughing in his bedroom about Quilp the dwarf. I think it was at Ardchullarie, that your grandfather Campbell courted sweet faced Anna Porteous. You know how sweet her face is still, as granny Campbell.

MR GLEIG

Visits were also paid by mother to the Rev. Robert Gleig, son of the Bishop. [71] He had been in the army, and then took Holy Orders, and finally through the influence of his friend the great Duke of Wellington, became Chaplain General of the Forces. It was on one of these visits, when the Gleigs were in an English Rectory, that mother was amused by a mistake of a footman. "John", said Mrs Gleig at lunch, "take these tartlets and heat them." As the tartlets did not appear, she rang the bell, and asked John for them. "Ma'am, said he aghast, "you told me to take them and heat them", and he had actually eaten them!

Mr Gleig preached very impressively, and once at Chelsea Hospital when he was preaching about the wars of Joshua, so graphic were his descriptions, old soldier that he was, that Mother said he roused the old pensioners to enthusiasm, and they thumped the floor with their wooden legs, with delight. Mr Gleig wrote several good handbooks on various subjects for schools, also one or two novels.

DUEL BETWEEN THE DUKE OF WELLINGTON AND LORD WINCHELSEA

The "Iron Duke" and the Earl of Winchelsea quarrelled, and fought a duel. I forget what they fell out about, but they made it up after the duel; and to

70   1841.

71   Reverend Robert Gleig (1796-1888), novelist.

show the world that they were reconciled, Lord Winchelsea gave a great party. Among the guests, were Uncle Duthie and Mother. She naturally wanted to see the Great Duke, and looked about for some imposing personage. At that moment, a small insignificant looking man as she thought, in a plain dark uniform, asked Uncle Duthie to introduce him to "Miss Murray." Much astonished was she as she shook hands with him to find that the "insignificant looking man" was the great conqueror, the Duke par excellence.[72]

DUCHESS OF KENT. PRINCESS VICTORIA

Once, when Mother was staying with Uncle and Aunt Duthie, they heard that the Duchess of Kent and her daughter Princess Victoria (now our dear Queen 1894) were to spend a night at an inn near. As Rector of the Parish (I forget which it was in Kent) Uncle Duthie went to receive and welcome them. And while the Duchess and her daughter dined, Mother and Aunt Duthie were taken by the landlady of the inn into the Duchess's bedroom, where they were interested in seeing the little bed in which the young Princess always slept. Not till she became Queen, did she have a separate room, so careful was the excellent mother about her daughter. Indeed, one of the Queens earliest remarks on her accession was, "Now I shall have a room of my own"! The little bed was, I think, blue and white. Mother amused herself trying on the Duchess's satin-lined cloak. She was always full of fun, and enjoyed everything.

ARCHBISHOP OF CANTERBURY

One of the visitors at Livelands in his boyhood, was Archibald Campbell Tait,[73] son of the proprietor of Harvieston Castle near Menstrie. He afterwards became Archbishop of Canterbury. Our dear old servant Jenny Welsh knew him when he used to come to the Bishop's; and I remember when I went into the kitchen at Park Terrace to tell her of his death, she, startled out of her exceedingly respectful manners, and remembering only the boy of other days, exclaimed "O me! is Airchie deed"!

It was on one of Mother's visits to the Duthies, that a man and woman brought their baby boy to be christened. "Name this child," said Uncle Duthie. "Zaphnappaaneah," (Joesph's name in Egypt) said the godmother. Uncle demurred, but they fell held firm. "But what shall you call him?", asked Mother of the baby's mother after the christening. "Oh Zap, miss" said she.

---

72 Arthur Wellesley (1769-1852), the 'Iron' Duke of Wellington and victor of Waterloo was an influential figure in early Victorian Britain.

73 1811-1882, consecrated Archbishop in 1868.

Another man, a draper of the name of Smith, said his child was to be christened "Sir John"! Uncle Duthie said he had no right to append a title, but the man angrily said the clergyman was bound to christen a child by whatever name its parents chose. Uncle Duthie, however, calmly poured the water on the little face, saying "John, I baptise thee etc."

Aunt Duthie's dress caught fire, and she would have been badly burnt but for Mother's presence of mind. Wrapping her in hearth rug and woollen table cover, she soon put out the flames, never heeding her own badly burnt hands, my dear, brave, unselfish mother! The right hand thumb must have been sprained in her exertions, because the joint was always large afterwards; and a favourite little ring given to her by Uncle Duthie, a forget-me-not, in blue turquoise, pearls, and diamond centre, had the diamond lost by the burning of the setting. This little ring mother gave to me not long before she left us, saying "I like it so much, I shall maybe sometimes ask you to give me a wearing of it." So I prize the little ring she liked so much.

Mother was exceedingly fond of music, and played with a brilliant touch. She used to play duets with Mrs Macdonald of Easter Livelands, when, as Mary Anne Horseman, she lived with her father at Springbank. Like many ladies of that time, she gave up her music when the cares of motherhood came upon her. Copying music was a great occupation in those days when music, like books, was dear, and not so plentiful as now.

She was also a great reader, devouring everything that came in her way. With Alick, she read Rollin's Ancient History, and Plutarch's Lives. I have heard her say that at that time those two books and White's Natural History of Selborne were her favourite reading. She drew and painted beautifully, and could take likenesses, such as your father does now, dear Isobel and Leslie. I have a specimen of her beautiful flower painting on rice paper, dated 1828. Above all things, she was an exquisite needle woman, and Mary Dow, the ladies maid at Livelands, has often told us how, when she went to call her in the morning, she found "Miss Murra", had been up and at her work by six o'clock.

Tall, slight, with dark brown hair, clear grey blue eyes, a perfect little head exquisitely poised, rather proudly carried, tiny, shell-like ears, and an altogether aristocratic appearance, she was no doubt much admired. But she "liked her freedom" as she told Mrs Pollok-Morris. As well as Mr Henderson, she had an admirer, Thomas Buchanan of Dowanhill. Why he did not propose to her, I know not, for that he loved her, was certain. But with the reserve of every member of the Dowanhill family, his only remark on her engagement to our father being announced, was "She need not have been in such a hurry!" Possibly she was his only love, for he died unmarried.

And after the lapse of many years, this little remark, unknown to her before it was told to Mother in 1887 at Meiklewood, where she and JA had gone to call on Mrs William Connel, an old Glasgow friend. With the frank garrulousness of extreme old age, she talked to Mother of Tom's love for her, and ended by repeating the one speech he made on the subject, whereat Mother blushed like a girl.

MEETING OF MY FATHER AND MOTHER

When my father first met my mother, I do not know, but I know it was at Dowanhill; but I do know from Aunt Eliza and Mrs Pollok-Morris, as well as from old Mary Dow, the maid, that long before he asked her to be his wife, the steadfast eyes of this pure, true, Christian Gentlemen grew glad at her coming; his firm hand clasped hers with an eager clasp; his great, strong heart throbbed with longing for her, whom after years of wedded love he could proudly tell Jane Anne, was "The only woman I ever loved!" And now, dear Isobel and Lesley, I have told you all I can about the Murrays of Livelands, I must begin the chronicles of the Wrights of Calder Park. To do this I must go back a trifle of 200 years!

1609 - 1643

THE WRIGHTS OF CALDER PARK

For the genealogy, I must refer you, my dear Isobel and Leslie, to Auntie Jean's "Tree Book", as I only undertake to tell you the stories of our family. There is an amusing one about a certain fair ancestress, Margaret Hamilton of Ferguslie, which I shall now tell you. About the year 1609, this Margaret married a John Wallace, descended from William Wallace of Elderslie and Jean Chalmer of Gadgirth, his wife. Through these Wallaces, we are descendants of Sir William Wallace. So you see, dear children, you have in you the blood of the two great Scottish patriots, Bruce on dear Granny's side, and Wallace on your grandfather's. Margaret Hamilton, Mrs Wallace, succeeded to the estate of Ferguslie on the death of her brother, and resumed her maiden name of Hamilton, her husband dropping his own and taking it too. He purchased Barr Castle in the parish of Lochwinnoch, Renfrewshire.

THE GUIDWIFE OF FERGUSLIE

Mrs Hamilton was either an Episcopalian or a Roman Catholic, and therefore refused to attend the services in the parish church of Paisley. In these stern days, there was no liberty of conscience so Margaret was taken to task for non church going. The first notice we have of this, occurs in the Records of the Presbytery of Paisley where it is noted that the Guidwife of Ferguslie, as she is styled, will not go to Church. The ministers then determined to go to her, and accordingly they visited her at Blackstoun near Paisley where she was then living. Poor Margaret! How they must have attacked her! It is recorded that they read and expounded the Scriptures to her. They also sang Psalms. I should like to know which Psalms they chose. I fear they would be of a denunciatory nature. But in spite of reading, expounding, and psalm singing, Margaret remained obdurate. So too did the ministers, and in the end they prevailed; for the next record states that on March 27th 1646 the Guidwife of Ferguslie "subscribes the confession of Faith and Covenent, and renounces Popery."

But she went not to church! So the ministers attacked her again. This time, they order her husband to force her to church, to bring to Paisley "by land or water to attend the preaching of the Word." All this persecution made Margaret very ill, and her husband sent a message to the Presbytery to say she could not be removed. Two members of that determined body were then dispatched to enquire into the truth of this. They reported "that she was very infirm, but that she had promised (poor persecuted woman!) to attend in twenty days albeit she should be carried on her bed." The next notice in the Presbytery books shows the result, - on May 8th 1647, Mr Henry Calvert, Minister of Paisley, reports that Margaret Hamilton, the Guidwife of Ferguslie, had come to the Kirk of Paisley, "carried on a bed." Truly these were the days of discipline!

THE HAMILTONS OF BARR CASTLE 1643-1700

This Margaret and her husband had a son, John Hamilton, who married in 1643 Agnes, daughter of William Cunninghame of Craigends. Their son John married Margaret, daughter of Colonel Hugh Cochran of Ferguslie. This Colonel Hugh Cochran was brother of the first Earl of Dundonald and uncle of Jean Cochran who married first John Graeme of Claverhouse, Viscount Dundee, and secondly Lord Kilsyth. John Hamilton and his wife Margaret Cochran built an addition to Barr Castle, and their initials are on the lintel of a window, IH-MC-1680. They had a son, Alexander, designated younger of Barr on the Role of Freeholders of Renfrewshire at the Union, 1707. He married in 1700, Margaret, daughter of John Hamilton of Udston, ancestor of Lord Belhaven.

MACDOWALLS OF CASTLE SEMPLE 1740

John and Margaret Hamilton had a daughter Margaret, (it seems to have been a favourite name of the Hamiltons of Barr!) and in 1740 she married John Macdowall of Park Hill. Park Hill, stood on rising ground on the right as you enter the gates of Castle Semple, and only the ruins of the house remain. John Macdowall acted as factor to his cousin, the laird of Castle Semple and Garthland, both places being in the parish of Lochwinnoch. But in later times, the Macdowalls sold Castle Semple to the Harveys (who still possess it in 1895) and retained only Garthland. I do not know when the Hamiltons ceased to possess Barr Castle, but the dear old place is in ruins.

I always like to go to look at it. I went there for the last time in the summer of 1882. Things were sorrowful then, Aunt Eliza was laid to rest in the old kirkyard and, Aunt Margaret was so old and feeble that I knew she must soon follow. So I said goodbye to the ruined castle, sorrowfully, and turned away. The great trees cast flickering shadows across the grass, the grass was white with daisies. How many little Margarets, daisies themselves, had gathered the pretty flowers, and played under the trees. Our people for centuries possessed lands in Renfrewshire, not one foot of it all do we possess now, only the graves in the old kirkyard of Lochwinnoch.

MARRIAGE OF JEAN MACDOWALL AND JAMES WRIGHT

The only child of John and Margaret Macdowall was a daughter named Jean, who married James Wright, whose mother (it is thought) was a Speirs of Elderslie. He was believed to be a Virginian merchant, and lived in Glasgow, where he possessed many houses near The Cross of that City, which gave him a right to eleven "lairs", in the old burial ground of the cathedral. He was also a Burgess of Glasgow. They had two children, William and James. James died young. William was a delicate child, and did not thrive in Glasgow, so he was sent to his grandparents at Park Hill, with his nurse Janet Hall. There he was much petted and loved. He remembered being dressed in black velvet with white lace. His mother must have been very young when she married, as he was born in Glasgow in 1760 just twenty years after his grandparents were married! Mr and Mrs Wright went to London, and Mr. Wright died of fever either there or in New York (our aunts could not remember which, nor could they give the date of Mrs Wright's death, but no doubt she died young.)

WILLIAM WRIGHT'S ONLY REMEMBERANCE OF HIS MOTHER

When William was about three years old, he remembered his mother coming to Park Hill; but he did not see her, because he had been taken by a manservant named Archie Malcolm, and hidden in a loft, whether by design or accident it is not known. There was an idea that Aunt Margaret had, that the mother wanted to take the child with her to London, and that the grandparents were unwilling to part with him. If that is so, then they carried their point. All little William remembered, was, seeing a lady in a yellow chariot drive up to the house, and he was told by the servant that the lady was his mother. He remembered the chariot going round the outside of the wood. And that is all he knew of his mother, for it was her last visit to Park Hill.

He was very tenderly and carefully brought up by his grandparents; and as soon as he was old enough, they gave him the choice of a profession. The cotton-spinning business was then at its height, and there being excellent water-power in Lochwinnoch, the Calder Park mill was built by a Mr Burns from England, Mr Houstoun of Johnstone Castle, and some of the Macdowalls. The managing partner was Mr Burns, and he agreed to teach young William Wright (our grandfather) the business. When he had learnt it thoroughly, and proved himself trustworthy, Mr Burns returned to England. William after some time bought the mill, and at first had a Mr Sharp as partner. He used to ride between this mill and the one at Cartside.[74] Cartside Mill was the oldest mill in Scotland. Calder Park Mill, burnt some years ago, ranked next in age. We have a piece of a dress of Jean Macdowall, Mrs Wright our great grandmother, a rich cream-coloured brocade, with bunches of green leaves and flowers.

MARRIAGE OF WILLIAM WRIGHT AND MARGARET WILSON

On the 29th of August 1783, our grandfather William Wright married Margaret Wilson of Bourtrees and Netherhouses. The marriage took place at Bourtrees.[75] The bride was a beauty, and as good as she was bonny. She was only eighteen. The bridegroom was twenty-three. He was slight and delicate looking but possessed of great personal dignity, and his word was law in the village of Lochwinnoch. Mrs Logan, the post-mistress told me that if he suspected the least demur in carrying out his orders he would say calmly, "I am Mr Wright, I have said it", and the thing was done. In our democratic days this sounds some what autocratic; but he was a just man, and an upright, and much beloved and respected, and it was considered an honour to be one of his mill-workers.[76]

I must tell you another little instance of his personal influence, it was then considered extremely wrong to take a walk on Sunday, (the Sabbath day, as our forefathers called it). One fine Sunday in summer, the minister of Lochwinnoch found that some of the villagers were out walking. Calder Glen is very lovely, (Ah me, that I could see it again!) and the miscreants had wandered up beyond the dam to enjoy its beauty. Possibly the minister was doubtful of his power over his parishioners, so he went in hot haste to our grandfather. Off the two went, and it is said that our grandfather simply ordered them to go home, and they went! We live in changed times. "But the old order changeth yielding place to new and God, fulfils Himself in many ways."

JANET COCHRAN OF BARCOSH

Margaret Wilson's mother was Janet Cochran of Barcosh. She was born in 1736 or 1737, and married in 1758, William Wilson of Bourtrees. Our father's

---

74 On the banks of the River Cart, and powered by water. Water powered cotton spinning mills were built in various places in Scotland from the late 1770s, the most famous being New Lanark (1786).

75 Bourtrees, Netherhouses, Barcosh, and Garthlands are all in the parish of Lochwinnoch between Howwood and Beith.

76 They went on strike in 1810.

cousin Mrs Lyons often spoke of her worth and great beauty. She had three brothers, one of them was drowned while bathing in the Cart near Paisley. She remembered when she was visiting at a Bailie Cochran's house in Paisley, that a bell-man used to go through the town on certain days, shouting out that letters were to be sent to Glasgow or Edinburgh that day. What a scrimmage the ringing of that bell could cause to people unaccustomed to dash off hasty notes as we do now! I fancy not very many would be written by the "Paisley bodies" of that time. The inhabitants of Edinburgh, Glasgow and Paisley, were then and for years after respectively called, "Edinburgh People", "Glasgow Folk", "Paisley Bodies."

Aunt Margaret used to relate with much amusement a story of some great entertainment given by some Paisley people who had risen in the world. "The Bodies", said she, "wanted to be hospitable, and pressed their guests to eat, but neither host nor hostess had the least idea what to call the fine dishes, so they contented themselves with saying, 'Will you taste this, O do try that,' O the poor "Bodies", ended she, laughing merrily. That "nous avons change tout cela", and no doubt the name of "Paisley Bodies" is forgotten.[77]

But I must return to my great grandmother Janet Cochran. The Sunday after her marriage to William Wilson, she and her husband went to the old parish church at Lochwinnoch of which only the belfry remains, and it is said that the young bride caused quite a sensation because of her great beauty, and also because she wore for the first time a bonnet. No one else in the church that day was similarly adorned but the lady of Castle Semple. It would appear that bonnets were then a novelty in Renfrewshire. Ladies dressed their hair very high, many had wigs, and wore marvellous headdresses or turbans on the top thereof. Girls of the working class wore the maidens "snood", and their shawls over their heads; elderly women wore "mutches."

The first dinner party Mr and Mrs Wilson went to after their marriage was at Barr Castle. Not long after they were married, Janet invited her husband's cousins the Wilsons of Bowfield to tea; and after tea, she and her husband "convoyed" (as we say in Scotland) the cousins part of the way home. Greatly distressed was the bonny bride on her return home, to find that a dog or cat had jumped on the table, and overturned it, breaking all her pretty wedding china.

Janet was a splendid horse woman. Like most people of her time, she was very superstitious. One day she rode alone from Bourtrees to Barcosh to see someone who was ill. On the way back, she and her horse were startled by a loud report in the sky right over her head. She was soon followed by a servant, who told her the sick friend at Barcosh had died suddenly. On

---

77 Paisley People are still called 'bodies' or 'buddies' and there are various other explanations. Professor John Wilson, 'Christopher North' of literary fame who was a native of Paisley referred in a speech to Paisley having 'so many souls'. His friend Thomas Campbell leaned forward and whispered, "<u>bodies</u>, you mean!" The phrase 'nous avons change tout cela' - 'we have changed all that' - is a famous ironical remark from a play by Moliere.

enquiry Janet found that the death took place at the very time she heard the noise.

William Wilson, Janet's husband, was a kind-hearted, easy-going man. He inherited Bourtrees from his father (the "bourtree" is a Scottish name for the elder tree). He was fond of company, and his friends took advantage of his good nature, and borrowed money from him, and got him to put his name to bills. In the end he had to sell Bourtrees, they then went to live at Calderhaugh in Lochwinnoch. His great friend was Macdowell of Garthland, and he dined there very often.

THROWING THE PRINCE OF WALES OUT OF A WINDOW

This Laird of Garthland was a friend of the Prince of Wales, afterwards King George IV. The Prince offered to visit Garthland incognito. He spent one night there, and a few of the neighbouring gentlemen were invited to meet him, among them our great grandfather William Wilson. All the guests were pledged to secrecy as to the rank of the guest of the evening. A very merry party it was, but in the course of the entertainment, the Prince who was very drunk, grew angry with something, or someone. The others, forgetting his rank, and being muddled themselves, seized him and promptly landed him outside the window on the grass. Fortunately it was a low window. Our great grandfather was always very reticent about the proceedings of that evening, but he said that he helped to pull the Prince in again. (Jane Anne knows the window out of which he was thrown). With all his faults, the Prince was good natured, so the affair was kept quiet.

The Crest of our Wilsons is a wolf resting on its hind legs, with forepaws extended. We have a bit of a dress of your great grandmother Mrs Wilson, a rich old gold brocade, with bunches of flowers. An easy chair at Calder Park was covered with this brocade, and much prized by Aunt Margaret, who was greatly attached to her grandmother. It is now in the possession of the Cunninghams at 43 Queen Street, Edinburgh.

DEATH OF WILLIAM WILSON 1808, JANET WILSON

Our great-grandfather died at Calderhaugh in 1808, aged 74; and our great grandmother continued to live there till her death in 1825. Aunt Margaret was a great favourite of her grandmother's, and spent the last year of her life with her, and received several presents from her, amongst others a feather bed, then considered a very necessary article. Indeed a bride was not considered properly dowered, unless she went to her husband with a large supply of fine linen sheets, blankets, counter-panes, table-linen and a feather bed. And when your dear Mother was engaged to be married, my dear children, Grannie and I were consulting about ways and means to get her trousseau, Grannie said, "Well, there's one thing I'm determined about, and that is, she must have some sheets and a feather bed."

Our great grandmother used to receive some money once or twice a year. On these occasions, she summoned all her daughters, and divided the money amongst them. No doubt that was a very happy day at Calderhaugh, the good old mother giving, and the daughters receiving. It must have been a good sum too, for Aunt Margaret remembered her mother coming home with fifty pounds. A favourite book of our great grandmother's was Isaac Ambroise's "Looking unto Jesus"; and Aunt Margaret told me that she never went to bed without repeating the beautiful hymn, "Jesus Lover of my Soul." The idea for this hymn was suggested to Charles Wesley (1707-1788) by a little bird flying into his study to take refuge from a hawk. Aunt Margaret always repeated this hymn when she went to bed too. And as she lay dying in 1882, I used to hear her say it to herself night after night. In place of "hangs my helpless soul on Thee", she said "my weary soul", and there was a little wistful intimation in that line, as if she was a little tired, and would be glad to "fall asleep", dear Aunt Margaret! A guinea, given to our father by his grandmother of whom he was very fond, and treasured by him, is among the family records. Cousin John Freeland, then a tiny child always got a shilling or half a crown from her when he was taken to Calderhaugh. In those provident days, he was not allowed to spend the money, it was kept for him by our grandmother Mrs Wright.

CALDER PARK

As I said previously, our grandparents, William Wright and Margaret Wilson were married in 1783. They lived first in a house called Kildale near the mill, and there their 13 children were born. But houses were built close to it, so they moved to Calder Park, sometime after 1807. Calder Park was a small house, and my grandfather wished to build another in the high field above it, or in one of the fields on a line with it. He had all the plans prepared. But grandmother thought the site of the old house was sheltered, and urged him to add to it instead. This, perhaps, was unwise, the house being so old; but he agreed to her wish, and made the addition, at perhaps at much cost as building a new one. It had a beautiful old fashioned garden, at the foot of which, shaded by a large tree, ran the River Calder. There was a green lattice-work arbour under some great trees, where grandmother loved to sit; and on the river bank, were seats, where also, she was often to be found.

THE CHILDREN AT CALDER PARK

Of the 13 children of our grandparents, 4 died very young; their names were Jane, John, Robert and Alexander. The 9 who lived to grow up were, Janet, Mrs Freeland, born in 1784, died in 1822. Her son John born June 26 1819 now Free Church Minister of Innerwick, East Lothian (1895) was taken to Calder Park as a baby, and brought up by his grandmother and Aunt Margaret. William, born 1786, was married to Margaret Auchenclose about 1816. She died in 1820, and Uncle William went to America. His boy, William, was left at Calder Park. Uncle William married again in America and died there in 1868. James, our dear father, born Sept. 29th 1789. There was some thought of calling him Humphrey, but it was given up for James. He was no doubt baptised by Mr James Steven, then, and till 1801, parish minister of Lochwinnoch. Another Jane was born on April 3rd 1794.

THE CHILDREN AT CALDER PARK

Apparently our grandparents clung to the family names; and I think it was a nice feeling of regard for his mother's memory, that made grandfather when his first little Jane died, call another child by the same name. "Jeans" were becoming "Janes" by this time! And the carefully preserving a bit of his mother's dress, an unusual thing for a man to do, showed a tender feeling for the mother whom he had never seen since he was about 3 years old. The next child, Margaret, was their seventh child, born at 7 o'clock in the morning on the 7th May 1796. In after years, we used to tell Aunt Margaret that is why she was so good, seven being the number of perfection. She was the home-daughter, greatly loved by her mother whose namesake she was. "The others liked to go about and visit their friends", she often told us, "but I, my dears, I stayed with my mother"; and the last year or two of her life, she would say "You won't leave me, Margaret my dear?" and I said "Never!"

AUNT ELIZA BORN OCTOBER 18TH 1807

Agnes was born, August 12th 1798. She married the Rev. James Munro, afterwards Free Church Minister of Rutherglen. They had an only child, Margaret Wilson. Between Aunt Margaret and Aunt Agnes there was a very strong affection, and after the marriage of the latter, a weekly letter, nay volume, never failed, on both sides. Twins, John and Mary were born Nov. 28th 1801. And the last child was born October 18th 1807. The family names were all used up by her twelve brothers and sisters, and she was to have been christened Elizabeth; but in the end, received the then fashionable name of Eliza. All our aunts were dear and good in their several ways. All were loved by us, their nieces. But of Aunt Eliza, dear Aunt Eliza, I quote these words, reverently, lovingly, thankfully, as appropriate to her dear memory:-

> *"Through such souls alone,*
> *God stooping, shows sufficient of His Light*
> *For us in the dark to to rise by."*
> *(From the "The Ring and the Book")*

And not long ago, when I was ill, I dreamt as I so often do, that I was at Calder Park. This time I was standing by Aunt Eliza, kissing her dear, dead face, tears raining down my face, as I sobbed aloud, "O God, I thank Thee, I thank Thee, for Aunt Eliza!" I suppose I must have awaked as I said this; but I know that in full consciousness, with tear-filled eyes I sat up in bed, and said again, "God! I thank Thee for giving us Aunt Eliza." Does she know now how we loved her, how we love her still? Is she allowed to whisper good thoughts to us when we are tempted, a comforting one when we are sad? Lord God, Thou knowest! But you, Jane Anne and Mary, will join with me in saying, that deep in our hearts, enshrined in all that is holiest and best in us, is the dear memory of Aunt Eliza. She was not perfect. I do not say that she was, though I myself, cannot recall a fault in her. She had her little peculiarities no doubt. She was neither beautiful nor handsome, so it was not appearance that attracted the love of kinsfolk and friends, servants, and villagers alike to her. It must have been her grace of mind, her quick sympathy, her loving heart. And then how merry she was, how she would laugh at our jokes and stories, though sorrow and suffering during long long years were hers in no ordinary degree. She and my father, though widely separated in age, were devoted to one another. "I wonder you never married, " I said once to her with the cheerful frankness of youth which knows not that even in elderly people there are old wounds that never heal. In Aunt Eliza's case there were no wounds, however. "My dear", said she laughing merrily, "I never could have married because your Papa was my ideal, and I never saw a man that could come up to him."

THE DAVIDSONS IN GLEN ROSA

But I am digressing. I must go back to the story of the young family at Calder Park, and tell about their nurse. Before my grandfather was married, he used often to go to Arran for fishing. He lodged in the Davidsons' house at the entrance of Glen Rosa, "Glen Rosie" as the old Arran people called it. The Davidsons were all exceedingly handsome. One of them, Lizzie, as a very old woman, living with her brother Peter and his daughters in the Free Church Manse at Brodick, used to like to tell us about our grandfather. "He was a very grand old gentleman", she said in her Highland accent, "and I was very fond of him." She was little more than a child at the time, and someone had given her a rosy apple. Apples were scarce in Arran, there were no orchards, and but few fruit trees except in the Castle gardens. So Lizzie prized her apple, and made up her mind to give it to Mr Wright. She was standing among the corn, waiting for him, when he came along with a friend, and she thrust the apply shyly into his hand. "Is this for me?" he said kindly, and he took the apple and turned it over, saying to his friend, she hasn't even put her teeth to it to taste it." But poor Lizzie overheard the remark, and the proud Highland heart was hurt, and she hid herself among the corn, and cried. "Did he think," said she to us "that I would have touched it when I meant it for him!"

JENNY DAVIDSON, THE NURSE AT CALDER PARK

When our grandfather had children of his own, he sent to Arran for Jenny Davidson, Lizzie's sister to be their nurse. In Arran, she had never worn such a thing as a bonnet, but some time after her arrival at Lochwinnoch, she of course got one to be like the other people. News of this reached her ain folk in Arran, and they sternly remonstrated with Jenny for going in for what they called "the vanities of the world." But Jenny continued to wear her bonnet, and was generally known as "Mrs Wright's pretty servant." Jenny's brother Peter became a minister, and once when he came to see her, my grandmother did not know what to do; for as the nurse's brother, the kitchen was the place for him, but in virtue of his office of minister of the gospel, the dining room. The latter was decided on, and no doubt greatly to Peter's embarrassment, he was asked to join the family at tea. It was the first time he had ever tasted tea, and he drank a cupful straight off, saying as he set the cup down, "I'll no tak' ony mair o'that whey", (pronounced like why). Poor Peter, he thought it very odd whey, and must have feared he was being poisoned.

Jenny was a disciplinarian. My father never could make his mug of milk last out till his porridge was eaten. He generally found himself milkless before he was half done. "Jenny, my milk's done" he would say sadly. "Then tell the porridge the milk has gone before it," answered Jenny, and not another drop did he get. In her old age, when Jenny, as Mrs Barr, was living in Ardrossan, I remember going with our father to see her. She had a nice house, and was quite like an old lady. "Jenny", said my father mischievously, "I've been telling the children that you would not give me enough milk for my porridge." "Oh sir, you shouldn't tell them such stories," said she. Our father was very good to his old nurse, and when she was left a widow, he helped her family on in the world. Her son, Angus, was a clerk in his office, and I remember him as a gentle, quiet man, grieving about his little boy whose leg had to be taken off.

AUNT JANET

During Jenny's reign at Calder Park, the children had measles. Aunt Janet and our father were ill in the same room, and once when Jenny had been called away for a few minutes, Janet sighed, "O how hot I am!." "Never mind, Janet," said our father soothingly, "I'll soon make you cool." Which he did, effectively. For he caught up the bellows and puffed vigorously at her, and the rash was all driven in, and poor Janet was seriously ill for a long time after. There is a miniature of Janet, now in the possession of her grand daughter Emily Freeland, which represents her as a very pretty young girl, blue-eyed, fair complexioned, with masses of rich brown hair. I have a bracelet of her hair, which Aunt Jane often wore with a handsome gold clasp set with aquamarine stones. When Janet let her hair down, it was a perfect veil to her, she could sit on it, our aunts said.

HALF-WITTED PEOPLE

There were one or two half-witted people, "naturals" they were called, in the village, who greatly amused the young people. One of them had an immense admiration for Aunt Margaret, and prefaced every remark he made to her with deep bows, calling her "Lady Margaret, Madam, Mum," and then saying what he wanted. Another, Daft Willie, turned into rhyme everything that was said to him. His cleverness in this way was wonderful. I have heard my father say that he never hesitated over the most out of the way sentence.

LORD CRAWFORD AND LORD BOYD

Lord Crawford and his son, Lord Boyd, determined to puzzle him, and one day said "Beh-eh-eh"! in his face, imitating the roaring of a bull. "There, Willie, that will puzzle you!", but Willie was equal to the occasion. Without the least hesitation he said:-

> *"The Earl of Crawford and Lord Boyd,*
> *Of grace and manners, they are void;*
> *For, like a bull among the kye,*
> *They "Beh" to folk as they gae bye."*

And scornfully turned Willie away; but Lord Crawford and his son delighted with his ready wit, paid him well, and told the story far and near. Poor Willie, his desires were humble, and easily satisfied. "What is your idea of perfect happiness?" my father asked him once. "Eh, sir, just to shiggie shoo (ie swing) on a gate a' day, and to hae parritch and cream to my supper at nicht." My father gave him something to get the parritch and cream, and as to the gate, it would not be far to seek.

"YOUNG MEN WHEN YE A COURTING GO"

The precentor of the village church wanted to improve the singing, and got up a class of young men to practise the psalms. My father had a fine tenor voice, and sang well, so he went to the class. The precentor thought it irreverent to sing holy words while they were practising the psalm tunes, so he chose a secular song. His choice was certainly singular; and the result was, that never was that particular psalm tune sung, without each of the young men, remembering the odd words. As it was a "repeating tune" that is, one where the last line of each verse is repeated, the effect must have been ludicrous. This is what they sang;

> *"Young men, when ye a courting go,*
> *The guidwife's favour crave;*
> *And when the kebbock does gang dune,*
> *Tak' ye a moderate sha-a-a-ave*
> *Tak' ye a moderate shave."*
> *(kebbock means a cheese, shave a slice).*

MODES OF TRAVEL

My father saw all the funny bits of life and enjoyed them immensely. Travelling in a stagecoach with two old ladies he was amused at the way they sat stiffly bolt upright, each twirling her thumbs, in solemn silence. It was in autumn just after the fruit-preserving season, and the making of jams and jellies was of immense importance to all good housewives. When the coach stopped at a wayside inn, one old woman said to the other solemnly, "Hae ye been haupy (happy) in yer jeel?" (jelly) And was duly answered thereof, whereupon they twirled their thumbs again, and made no further remark. By the way, that makes me wonder, do old women twirl their thumbs now? Menie Mackenzie used to do it. So too did sweet old Mrs Stavenhagen, she use to twirl them first one way, and then the other as if they had grown giddy.

LOVE OF MUSIC

They were all fond of music. Aunt Eliza painted nicely, and was clever in everything, a good French scholar, and interested in all scientific things. Uncle John painted well in oils, indeed he was too fond of art, and spent too much money in buying pictures.

My father had a story about a man in the village who was wooing a fair maid. She was hard to win. "O if ye'll marry me," said he "I'll promise to tak' ye to see every hanging there is in Paisley!" People could not have been squeamish then as to the sights they saw! Hangings were very frequent, a man would be hanged even for a small theft. My father went once to tea in a Quaker's house. He was offered some cake, and refused it, then said "I think I shall change my mind, and take a piece." "Thou shalt not tell a lie in my house", said the Quaker sternly. Change of mind is not allowed by them.

VISITS TO ARRAN

My grandfather's love of Arran continued, and he took his family often there in the summer time. There were then only small sailing vessels, or revenue cutters, but they all, Aunt Margaret especially, loved the sea. They went to a place in Arran beyond Lamlash, called Ben Lister. We seem to have love of Arran inherent in us. As the years went on, Uncle William went into business in Glasgow. My father went there in 1810, and then began the honourable business career, which lasted till his death in 1860. At that sad time, Sir Michael Connal,[78] looking at Mary and me, remarked to my Mother, "These little girls, if they knew it, might be proud to walk down the streets of Glasgow, as the daughters of such a man." This was a pleasing tribute from one so uncompromisingly strict and upright as Sir Michael was in all his dealings. My father was 5ft 11in, fair skinned, with blue eyes, and a good figure. He was exceedingly pleasant and genial. Mother told me she had never seen a frown on his face during all her married life. Anyone looking at him would have trusted him. The fact of the policeman in London readily letting him go close to the Queen, is a proof of this.

---

78 Sir Michael Connal (1818-1893) of Park Hall and Arngomery, grandson of Michael Connal, cloth merchant and three times Provost of Stirling who died in 1812.

It was in the early days of her reign, and the dear Queen was unpopular, because of the sad story of Lady Flora Hastings.[79] My father saw a crowd somewhere near Constitution Hill, and was told that Her Majesty was expected to pass that way. He said to a policeman that he wanted to raise a cheer for her as she passed, and the man arranged that he got to the front of the crowd, and in the end so near the Queen that he could have touched her. She was riding a white horse, and looked sad, and not a cheer came from the crowd. As she came to where my father stood the policemen said, "Now, sir", and he stepping forward, called out as loudly as he could, "God in Heaven bless and preserve your majesty!". Those standing near, and a few in the crowd, took up the cheer: my dear, loyal father said he never forgot the grateful look in the Queen's eyes as she bowed to him. Poor young Queen, hers was not a bed of roses at that time.

THE HOUSEHOLD AT ST VINCENT STREET

When my father went to Glasgow, he lived in Virginia Street till he took possession in 1825 of 225 St Vincent Street. This house he bought while it was in course of being built, it was as far on as the beginning of the dining room windows and the rest of the building was done under his direction, nurseries being added in after years. Aunt Jane kept house for him until his marriage, and they were soon joined by Aunt Eliza, and cousins John Freeland and William Wright, all three being educated in Glasgow, the two last being entirely at my father's expense. For Uncle William, William's father, was a great source of sorrow to his family, and especially to his brother James. His wife died about 1820 and in 1826 or 1827, he went to America. He was disinherited by his father. I am glad to be able to say that he did well in the new country, married a Miss Hood by whom he had a son and daughter, and died "a respected citizen" in 1868. John Freeland lived 10 years under my father's roof, and in 1840 was sent by him to Edinburgh to finish his study for the ministry under Dr Chalmers and Dr Welsh. William Wright was sent to Australia, not as a penniless lad to work his way, but equipped in all respects as if he had been a son instead of a nephew. Another inmate of 225 St Vincent Street was Uncle John, gay, merry, picture-loving Uncle John, and my father must have had his hands full with such a houseful. The dinner hour at that time was 5 o'clock (how odd that sounds now!). Tea was at 8, and after that the two brothers went back to the office till 9, as the London Mail came in between 7 and 8. Aunt Jane made a capital house-mistress.

There was plenty of money, cotton being then a flourishing business, and

---

79 In 1839, Lady Flora Hastings was ostracised by Queen Victoria's court in the mistaken belief that the tumour (of which she subsequently died) was an extra-marital pregnancy. The affair made Queen Victoria deeply unpopular.

the young people enjoyed seeing their friends, of whom they had many. Aunt Jane liked to rule, so the cares of the household did not oppress her; it is said she sometimes tried to rule the younger members more than they quite liked, but they all pulled together wonderfully well. Aunt Jane was tall, slight and handsome, with bright eyes and brilliant complexion. She was exceedingly popular, and had many admirers, but she liked her liberty, and her position as mistress of my father's house.

AUNT JANE AND DR BURNS OF TORONTO

It was a pity that she did not marry Mr Burns, Minister of Paisley, and afterwards of Toronto, where he became Dr Burns, and was highly esteemed. Though she refused him, I fancy she regretted it afterwards, from a little thing that happened at Calder Park not very long before her death. It was after tea, and we were still sitting round the table; and something was said about the old Scots song "The Flowers of the Forest", that beautiful song about those who fell at Flodden, pathetic both in words and music.

Aunt Margaret began to sing it. "O Margaret, stop," Aunt Jane said, "You know I can never hear that without greeting." I don't think Aunt Margaret heard her for she finished the verse, and turning to me said, "You see my dear, that song makes me think of Dr Burns of Toronto, the one our Jane ought to have married. It was a great pity she did not take him," she continued with reminiscent garrulousness of old age "for I assure you, my dear, he was greatly in love with her." "Margaret, Margaret, stop, I can't bear you bringing up these old things," said poor Aunt Jane now really in tears, but trying to laugh; and I flew to her, and hugged her, and told her it was no wonder he wanted to marry her. Poor, dear Aunt Jane!

DR BURNS OF THE BARONY

This Dr Burns of Toronto, was brother of Dr Burns of the Barony Parish.[80] The parishioners of the Barony, till the old Barony Church (now pulled down, and another in its place) was built, worshipped in the crypt of Glasgow Cathedral. This was long before the restoration of the Cathedral, and the gloom of the crypt must have been appalling. It cannot have affected the high spirits of its minister, for, far and near, Dr Burns was noted for his genial, kindly nature, and his love of a joke.

It was the custom then, and for some time after our parents' marriage, to offer cake and wine to callers, just as we now give them afternoon tea. The lady of the house, after breakfast put two decanters, one of red, the other of white wine on a silver tray, with wine glasses, and a plate of daintily cut cake and shortbread. This was brought into the room everytime a friend

---

80 Dr John Burns (1743-1839) was minister of Barony for 65 years and wrote the entry for the First
    Statistical Account. Two of his sons became eminent surgeons.

called, and it would have been thought extremely inhospitable not to have done so. Aunt Jane and Aunt Eliza calling on Dr Burns, were as usual offered wine. There was not much in the decanters, and after each had had a glass, Dr Burns pressed them to have more, which of course they refused. "Well I did want you to take it," said he laughing "for then you know, I could have told everybody that two ladies called on me and each finished her bottle!" The old rogue!

ALLAN CUTHBERTSON

There was a Mr Allan Cuthbertson that Aunt Jane did not care for, and who rather pestered her with his company. She "settled" him innocently enough, but effectually. She was coming out of church after an evening sermon, and seizing my father's arm, as she thought, and hurrying him along a step or two, said, "Come away, James, I want to avoid that horrid Allan Cuthbertson." Looking up, she perceived that she was arm-in-arm with "horrid Allan Cuthbertson"!

EDWARD IRVING

The great Edward Irving, founder of the Catholic and Apostolic Church was a great friend of our people. He had then returned to Glasgow to die, and used to ride through the streets with a large cloak on, ill, and weary, and sad. Aunt Jane's bright ways, and kindly words, must have been a pleasure to the worn out, disappointed man. Some gossiping person remarked to Aunt Jane how fond he seemed to be of her, "But what will Mrs Irving say?" (Mrs Irving was a cold, unsympathetic woman). Aunt Jane's proud spirit was hurt. How much mischief is done by these gossips!

And next time she saw Edward Irving riding slowly towards her, his wife walking beside the horse, she turned hastily down another street to avoid meeting them, and as she did so, saw him look surprised and sorry. The look haunted her and she felt vexed with herself for not speaking to him. Later, she grieved over it, for she never saw him again. Many mourned for Edward Irving, he had a singular power of fascination.[81] Thirty years after his death, Doctor Rainy could not speak of him without tears in his eyes; and he was by no means an emotional man, and must, in the course of his long medical practice, have been at many deathbeds.

RADICAL RISING

When the Radical Rising took place in the West,[82] my father joined the Corps called "The Sharp Shooters." The colonel highly commended him for

81 Edward Irving (1792-1834) was one of the most charismatic churchmen of his day. He married Isabella Martin after a seven year engagement in 1823, although he had been in love with Jane Welsh (who later married his friend, Thomas Carlyle) from 1821. The gossip of the time caused him great hurt and this story adds poignancy to his sad personal life.

his strict attention to his duties, and complimented him on his soldierly appearance, saying he was "fit to command a regiment." Some of the officers' wives were not as patriotic as their husbands, and when a report came that the rebels were at hand, and the men were ordered out, one or two failed to appear, because their wives had hidden their trousers! How my father use to laugh when he told this story!

RIDING SCHOOL

He was fond of riding, and had a horse called Jess. He went to a riding school in Glasgow; and the master after seeing him make his horse go over a bar that none of the other riders would attempt, said, "Mr Wright, there is nothing that I can teach you, you are a perfect horseman." Aunt Eliza told me this, with pride.

Our grandparents and aunts sometimes went to Bridge of Allan, and lodged in the farm on the left hand side of the road as you go from Causewayhead to Bridge of Allan. The farmer's name was Clayton. The only time mother ever saw my grandfather was during one of these visits. He had been into Stirling to see a dentist,[83] and was walking back to the farm, holding a handkerchief to his face. It was the only time he had ever had toothache. My father's teeth were beautiful. He never had toothache, and I believe never lost a tooth, so not doubt Mary and I inherit our strong teeth from him.

GRANDFATHER DIES AT CALDER PARK

Grandfather died at Calder Park on the 10th of March, 1829. When he was very ill, he sent Aunt Margaret to his private room at the Mill to fetch his desk[84] and papers. She told me that as she walked across the field carrying them, she said to herself that she should never be able to go there again without her father, it looked so deserted without him. And she never crossed its threshhold again.

AUNT AGNES' MARRIAGE

Aunt Agnes married the Rev. James Munro in 1837, and their only child, Margaret Wilson, was born in May 1840. Uncle Munro was an exceedingly handsome man. I do not think I ever saw a more picturesque head than his,

---

82 The Radical Rising of 1820 ended with the execution of James Wilson in Glasgow, and Baird and Hardie in Stirling. The Smith has the axe and cloak used by the Stirling executioner.

83 Stirling's first resident dentist was Leon Jablonski Platt, who started business in 1859. Before that, dentists were itinerant.

84 Presumably, a little portable writing desk. The Smith has a Victorian lap-top desk of this type, with compartments for pens, ink, and documents.

especially in old age. After the disruption,[85] he became Free Church Minister of Rutherglen near Glasgow.

UNCLE JOHN'S MARRIAGE

I do not know the date of Uncle John's marriage, but it took place before our parents were married. "Aunt John", we called her, because her name was Jane and she had to be distinguished from Aunt Jane. She was the daughter of a Mr Logan in Glasgow. Her own mother was dead, and she had an only sister to whom she was much attached. The two girls were married on the same day, standing on either side of their father who was paralysed, and unable to rise from his chair; the sister became the wife of Mr Williams of Tan-y-Greig in Wales.

Aunt John was a sweet little woman, with gentle, loving ways. She was extremely pretty. Some time after her marriage, a beggar woman stopped her, and asked her for money. As poor Aunt John put a coin into her hand, she saw that both the woman and the baby in her arms were in the infectious stage of small-pox. She hurried away, but soon sickened, and had a serious attack of the disease. Her pretty little face was pitted and seamed and her features thickened. So changed was she, that when our warm hearted father saw her for the first time after her recovery, he could only say a word or two, then had to go away to overcome his emotion. They had two sons, William, and David Logan.

VISITING THE POOR IN LOCHWINNOCH

We, in the end of this 19th century, hear a great deal of the endeavours made by charitable people to improve the conditions of the poor. But good people did very much for their poorer neighbours in former times, only it was more quietly done. I do not mean to depreciate the efforts that are made now, the guilds that are formed for supplying clothes, the great work of the Charity Organisations, etc., etc., but I do think it has become a sort of fashion for fine London ladies to go "slumming" as they call it, and that it is not done for pure love of God and their neighbours. But I may be wrong, and old-fashioned in my views. Much good was done in the village of Lochwinnoch by Aunt Margaret, Aunt Mary, and Aunt Eliza, but it was all so quiet; no talk of interesting cases, no excitement, no trumpeting forth their achievements. The poor were relieved, the sick visited, the children taught, but without the talk and fuss that so often we hear now. Mrs Logan, the village postmistress, told me that she had been in Aunt Mary's Sunday class for young women, "and we all looked up to her", she said, "if there was

---

85   The Disruption of 1843 which led to the creation of the Free Church of Scotland was a landmark event in Scottish church history. The Smith has the heel of the boot which the Reverend Dr Chalmers wore, when he walked out of the General Assembly to set up the Free Church. Purchased for 10 guineas, it was later presented to the Smith.

anything we wanted to know, no matter what, we used to say, "ask Miss Mary Wright, she's sure to know."

SCHOOL OF INDUSTRY

Aunt Mary had what she called her "School of Industry." She hired a large room in the village, and paid a mistress to teach the girls needlework and knitting. The mistress's name, when I was a child, was Mrs Caldwell, and we much enjoyed going to see the girls at work. How shocked Aunt Mary would be at the bad manners of children now! We were always treated by her scholars with the greatest respect. Before we left, the children used to sing hymns. And there was one which they always sang marching round the room, it is in Bateman's Hymn book, and is called "The Children's Marching Hymn",[86]

> *"There is a land of pure delight,*
> *Where saints immortal reign," etc.*

Aunt Eliza sold all her jewels, except the few that she had in constant use, and donated the money, a large sum, to buying Bibles for the village girls. I cannot remember the number she bought, but there were a great many, and Bibles could not be bought cheaply then. As to my father, he gave largely to every good work. Mrs Pollok-Morris told me that it was thought that he gave far too much. But I am proud to think that he was a willing giver, for does not he who gives to the poor "lend to the Lord?"

SPINNING AND WEAVING

All the house and table linen at Calder Park was handspun and handwoven. My grandmother kept four women in the village constantly employed spinning for the house. I remember seeing the remains of her own spinning wheel in the stable loft, and wishing it had not been so broken. Undergarments were all made of linen, and very fine linen too; and even after the use of cotton had become general, many ladies scorned to use it. To the end of their lives, our aunts refused to wear cotton, and my own Mother would only wear linen chemises. There were no machine-made trimmings then, and underlinen was trimmed with frills of fine cambric, exquisitely hemmed, and often (as in our aunts' case) edged with Valenciennes lace. There were many hand-loom weavers in the village, and the "click-clack" of the loom was a cheery sound as one passed along. But machinery destroyed that industry, and in late years I only remember one loom. Weavers were generally great politicians, and florists. I don't know about the politics, but I remember the village windows full of plants in fine condition.

---

86   Written by Isaac Watts (1674-1748).

The love of flowers has been very strong in some of our people, notably in Aunt Jane and Aunt Mary. Even in the "back green" in St Vincent Street, Aunt Jane cultivated flowers to a great extent, and indoors she had plants in pots. Now-a-days people have flowers in their houses whether they care for them or not, simply because it is the fashion; in those days only flower lovers had them. The little black table that I use for my plants, is the one that belonged to Aunt Jane. Aunt Mary made every bit of the ground at Calder Park gay with her flowers, under the walls, along the sides of the mill-lade, everywhere. How sweet the old-fashioned roses were! Grandmother's favourite was one called "The Maiden's Blush." There were great bushes of it at Calder Park, "my mother's rose", Aunt Margaret would say tenderly as she gathered one.

A newspaper was sent home once or twice a week by my father; and when it arrived, the bell was rung, and everybody assembled to hear the news. Letters came seldom, but the institution of the Penny Postage on January 10th 1840 soon made an immense change.

THE MARRIAGE OF JAMES WRIGHT - ISABELLA WORDIE MURRAY

And now, my dear Isobel and Lesley, I think I have told you all I remember about the Wrights of Calder Park. I must now tell you of the marriage of your grandparents.

From the time of my father's going to Glasgow, he had been a great friend of the Buchanans[87] of Dowanhill. Mr Buchanan was a cousin of our grandmother Jean Buchanan of Croy. Mr and Mrs Buchanan had four sons, George, Thomas, James and John, and one daughter Janet, Mrs Pollok-Morris of Craig. The sons were in business in Glasgow. Janet and Aunt Eliza were at school together. George was much in love with my Aunt Christian Jane Murray, and had she lived, would no doubt have married her. Of Thomas's love for my mother I have already written.

Neither of these two married. James married Wilhelmina Linbeg, a West Indian; and John married Jane Young. Dowanhill was then a long way out of Glasgow. Alas! like Kelvinside, Hamilton Park, and many other pretty places, it has now become part of the great whole, and is covered with terraces and crescents. It used to be pronounced Dowanhill, like "doo"; I think now they say it like "dow." I fancy the old house still stands.[88]

---

87 There were many wealthy Buchanans in Glasgow. In 1725, the Buchanan Society was formed to give charitable relief to aged and poor persons with that surname. The impressive building of the Buchanan Institution, Greenhead Street, adapted 1859 for the industrial training of destitute boys, still survives.

88 Dowanhill House is marked on the Glasgow Post Office Directory maps until 1900, bordered by Dowanhill, Hyndland, Lawrence and White Streets.

There was a large summer-house in the grounds, two stories high. It was called the Temple. Here Mr Paisley, tutor to the young Buchanans, used to retire to write his sermons. Mother, when she was visiting at Downanhill, delighted to knock vigorously on the door, and then run off to hide before the tutor opened it. Many years after, when he was parish minister of St Ninian's, and a doctor of Divinity, he and his second wife (Sabina Smith of Jordanhill, married January 1878) were lunching with us, and Mother asked him if he remembered the temple at Dowanhill, and how somebody used to belabour the door while he was studying, and told him it was she who was so mischievous. The old man was much amused. "Yes, I remember the mysterious knocks," he said, "but I never thought you were the culprit, Mrs Wright."

1840

My father often rode to Dowanhill before breakfast, had a feast of gooseberries, and rode home again. It was at Dowanhill that he met my Mother, and fell in love with her. She was his only love. Aunt Eliza and Cousin John Freeland said there were plenty of ladies who would have been very pleased to have married him, but he was not attracted to any one of them. He had many opportunities of meeting Mother at Dowanhill, and his love for her grew steadily, but I believe he wooed her a long time before he won her. He was so great a favourite at Dowanhill, that Mrs Buchanan was anxious for Mother to accept him, but Mother was very maidenly and reticent, and gave no sign of her feelings.

A great commotion got up by Mother's refusal to go to a dinner party to which my father and Aunt Jane had invited her. The day was Good Friday, and of course Mother, an Episcopalian, declined the invitation. Mrs Buchanan, who was very anxious for the match, was very angry with Mother for refusing, but she held firm. Mother gave me the little note written by my father, that caused such a stir. Our aunts had noticed our father's attachment for a long time, but as he said nothing, neither did they. They were all very glad about it, and thoroughly approved of it, but poor Aunt Jane naturally suffered a good deal. She had for so many years been the mistress of his house, she liked the town life, and had besides lost her place in the home circle at Calder Park from so many years of absence. It was then, I think, that she regretted casting off Dr Burns of Toronto. Poor dear Aunt Jane!

I said once to Aunt Eliza, "As you are all Presbyterians, were you not sorry Papa married an Episcopalian?." "My dear, no," said she earnestly," he could do no wrong in our eyes, O no, that never weighed with us at all." My father's attentions to Mother were known at Livelands, and Mary Dow, the lady's maid, who to the end of her days used to pay us a yearly visit, told us that she used to wonder if Mother would accept him. One day she went into the nursery at Livelands, and showed Mary the beautiful gold watch my father had given her. "O surely Miss Murray, you're going to take him now," said Mary. But Mother only laughed, and ran away.

My father proposed to her by letter. Aunt Eliza was his confidant in everything, but he did not even to her speak of his love. She told me that one morning at breakfast, she saw him turn over his letters, and hastily turn one over so that no one should see the hand writing. He looked so grave, that her loving heart ached for him, but he went off to his office without a word. They all went to a party that evening, and Aunt Eliza's anxiety increased when she saw he had something on his mind. She was his favourite sister, and always when they were out at night, she walked home with him, leaning on his arm. This night, as she put her arm through his, he said, "Eliza, I have something to tell you," and then stopped short. "James tell me, is it Miss Murray?", and then he told her all. But what weighed upon him, was how to tell Aunt Jane! and it was some time before he summoned courage to do so. The friends of both families were very much pleased. I copy here one or two letters, to show how much my dear father and mother were thought of by those who knew them.

LETTER FROM MRS BUCHANAN OF DOWANHILL 1840

From Mrs Buchanan of Dowanhill. Oct. 24. 1840

"I think I need not to tell you how utterly astonished I was last night in perusing your Papa's letter announcing your marriage with Mr Wright. I have to use an old adage that "faint heart never won fair lady." You know my opinion of the man.

He may have his weaknesses, who has not, but they lean to virtue's side. I am sure Mr Wright's wife will be adored, nay, spoiled by the Family, and if not, it must be a fault of her own. How have you carried on matters so quietly? We heard of no visits to Stirling, nor anything that could raise suspicion. How dared you to do so important a step without telling me! I have only to say that my most earnest wishes attend you for your happiness. To me it is another of Time's changes, but I ought to be thankful you are to be so near me. I shall never want a kind friend in my old age. Offer my regards to Mrs Murray and Jane, and also to Mr Murray. I feel for him in parting with you, though he has in times past not had much of your society, he may now see you oftener. He must have comfort in resigning you into the hands of a good man."

From the old lady's thankfulness at the prospect of having Mother near her, one sees that Mother's kind offices in mediating between her and her daughter were not forgotten. The "weaknesses" that leant to virtue's side in my father in the estimation of his character by the Buchanan family, were strong points in other people's eyes. He always gave a tenth of his money to the poor and the church, and indeed very much more. They thought he was foolish to give so much.

From Mr Buchanan of Dowanhill, Nov. 6 1840

"I need not add to what I have already said regarding the alliance you are about to form. The principle has been long among us, and is well known. I have not heard anything to his prejudice, while much is recorded of his useful and active benevolence. Miss Wright is a clever woman. The other members of the family are amiable, but not so much among us, and Mr Wright has long moved in good society."

You may remember, dear Isobel and Leslie, that your great, great grandmother Mrs Buchanan of Croy was this Mr Buchanan's first love, her daughter Jean was his ward, and naturally he was very fond of her daughter, your own dear Grannie.

LETTERS OF CONGRATULATION 1840

From George Buchanan. Glasgow. Nov. 13. 1840

"My dear Isabella, I have delayed about a week for a formal announcement from Mr Wright before venturing to congratulate you on the alliance which you are about to form, but seeing that it was not likely to come from his side I was obliged to ask him at last, which of us should wait till the other broke the ice. Having proceeded this far, I feel myself at liberty to wish you the long continued enjoyment of every happiness which the marriage state can confer, whatever boys and girls may fancy. You and I are by this time too well aware that perfect happiness is not to be expected in that, more than in any other situation in life, but from an intimate acquaintance with both parties, I entertain the utmost confidence that a larger share of it will fall to your lot than most people meet with during that pilgrimage."

JAMES BUCHANAN'S LETTER

From James Buchanan, Stanley, Perthshire. Nov. 14. 1840

"Many congratulations, my dear Isabella, on the auspicious event which your note of yesterday announces. I cordially wish you every possible happiness in the change, but I can do more, I can assure you of it. I have known Mr Wright long and intimately, and a better principled and better dispositioned man I would never desire to number among my friends and acquaintances. It must be a source of very great satisfaction to you to find that this union will have the approbation of all whose love and esteem you wish to preserve, for marriage as well as drink "sometimes parts good company." I shall take care not make the affair subject of conversation with anyone but my wife until I find it is publicly known, which, from what you write, I presume will soon be the case. Wilhemina sends her own congratulations, and with best regards to all at Livelands, I remain, my dear Isabella, very sincerely yours, James Buchanan."

After a time, marriage in this case, did rather "part good company." "Wilhemina", was a frivolous, worldly woman and Mother did not have as much intercourse with her as formally.

AUNT JANE'S LETTER TO MOTHER 1840

When my father announced his engagement, he wanted Aunt Jane to write at once to Mother, but a week at least passed before she did so. Though she had known of my father's attachment, still the thought of her own changed life did weigh a little heavily upon her at first, very naturally too. But her letter when she did write was just like the generous, warm-hearted nature she always had, and she was very much attached to Mother. I do think Mother was singularly fortunate in marrying into a family so kind and affectionate, and so free from all formality as the Calder Park household was. The most sisterly relations were maintained between her and them to the end of their lives. Mother told me she was always sure of a welcome and never waited to be invited to Calder Park. She would just write that she was going to them on a certain day, or that she would send us children and Nurse Margaret to them for change of air. And not very long before Aunt Eliza died, she wrote to Mother thanking her for some little gift which she had sent her, saying "But how much I have had to thank you for, my dear Isabella, since the day when I first called you my dear sister." Mother's dear face flushed with pleasure when she read this. In writing they always sign themselves "sister" to her, and she did the same to them. But I am digressing, dear Isobel and Leslie! This is Aunt Jane's letter:-

225, St Vincent Street Oct. 20th 1840

"My dear Miss Murray, I fear you think me unkind in not writing to you before this, but one trifle after another prevented me, besides I thought it prudent until after the end of last week. Rest assured, these alone are the reasons, and no want of interest. I have long had the pleasure of knowing you, and felt always a peculiar interest from the certainty that James was attached deeply to you although he never ever said so, but many little events combined to convince me that my opinion was not without foundation. But now all doubts and wonders have merged into realities, and from this time forth I must look upon you in a different light, and feel towards you as a sister. I am perfectly happy and delighted with James's choice, and if I know myself it will be my aim and desire to promote your and his happiness in any way within the compass of my power, and nothing will afford me greater happiness than that you always find you can confide in me as a sister. I am certain I speak the feelings of my mother and sisters, also indeed, of all the family. It will, I am sure, be all of their studies to make you happy among us. As to James, perhaps prudence would suggest silence, but duty to you, and also him, renders that impossible. I have long been associated with all his domestic affairs and know him better than any other can, and I need say no more when I tell you I do believe he never spent an evening out of his own house that he did not tell me where he was. He will, I am certain, be always kind and affectionate, but I am a sister, and must say no more. Above all, I trust the God of Providence and Grace will shower down upon you abundantly of His richest blessings, without that no connection in this world can yield real happiness. May we all be enabled to seek that blessing, sure that if we do seek it, it will be granted. If there is anything I can do, you can at all times command. My sisters, with all friends here, are well, Mrs Buchanan almost so again. With love, in which Eliza, who is at present with, us begs to join. Ever believe me, my dear Miss Murray, your sincerely attached Friend, Jane Wright."

It is pleasant to have to record, that the "sincerely attached friend", became soon the sincerely attached sister. Jane Lyons, my father's cousin, was very fond of dear Mother. She said to me more than once, "Your mother is an admirable woman, but what I admire most in her is her behaviour to her husband's people." Two charming little letters came from the little nieces, Jane and Margaret Duthie. One of them said, "I always thought you said you would never marry, but I daresay I shall like to sit on Uncle James's knee when I come to visit you in Glasgow."

UNCLE MACKENZIE'S LETTER

My grand-uncle, Captain Mackenzie wrote from Melville Place, Stirling, Jan. 18. 1841,

"My dear Isabella, your aunt said that on the present happy event occurring, the accompanying Tea Chest became yours. I fulfil what she said, assuring you that I feel confident in your happy prospects. God bless you. I remain your sincere and affectionate Uncle, Hugh Mackenzie."

THE "TEA POY"

The "Tea Chest" he speaks of, is the handsome rosewood one in our drawing room. The old name was "Tea Poy",[89] but they are never seen in modern drawing rooms, though possibly the fashion for them may be revived. The one we have in the dining-room was gained by Mother in a raffle. It was nice of Aunt Mackenzie to think of her niece's possible marriage, and to assign her a present. And it was nice of her old husband so long after her death to remember, and fulfil her wish.

---

89 Until pressure from the temperance movement led to the lowering of duty on tea, it was a highly expensive drink. The dried leaves were kept in a tea chest or teapoy in the drawing room, under lock and key.

After the engagement, my father went to pay a visit at Livelands. Mother had a bad cough that winter, and in the morning, he used to way-lay Mary Dow, the lady's maid, and say "Mary, how is your young lady's cough today?." And on answering, Mary found half a crown in her hand. "O", said she to me years after, "that was a grand cough for me, many a half crown I got just for telling him how Miss Murray was!" In a little diary of my grandmother's, we find -

"Friday, Oct. 16. 1840. Mr Wright from Glasgow, came here about 4 o'clock. Captain Mackenzie ("uncle") and Mr Campbell (your great-grandfather, dear children) asked to meet him. Oct. 17. Mr W. returned to Glasgow. He came to Livelands again Nov. 4. and also Nov. 18., and on the 19th he took the whole party for a drive by the foot of the hills, (Ochils) to Alloa, and there they had wine and cake at the inn, and drove home in time for dinner at 4 o'clock."

What an unearthly hour for dinner that seems to us! What immensely long evenings they spent after it!

On Dec. 7. my father and Aunt Jane went to Livelands. This was Aunt Jane's first visit there. The day after, he took them all for a drive to Dunmore and Airth, by Carron Hall and Kinnaird. He and Aunt Jane returned to Glasgow on the 9th. Uncle and Aunt Duthie came to Livelands on the 8th of Jan. to be there a few days before the wedding. His sister, Maria, came on the 15th. She was universally known then, and to the end of her days as "Aunt Maria." It was with her that your dear Grannie, Isobel and Leslie, danced a "fancy dance" when they were little girls.

THE WEDDING DAY JANUARY 19TH 1841

On the 18th, Aunt Jane and Aunt Eliza arrived. Next day, the wedding took place. It was a Tuesday. About 1 o'clock, two carriages arrived from Glasgow; in one, the bride groom, and "best man", George Buchanan, and Thomas Buchanan; in the other, Mr and Mrs John Wright, and Mr James Wilson of Carsehill, my father's cousin. On his arrival at Livelands, my father was not allowed to see his bride, that would have been considered unlucky, but he found time to write her a little note in pencil, which was taken to her just before the ceremony, when she had finished dressing. This little note in his beautiful handwriting, my Mother carefully kept in the dressing box which was one of the gifts given to her.

"Miss Murray, Livelands. My dear Isabella, here I am, safe and sound, and although I have not been permitted to see you, yet I had the pleasure of hearing your voice, and learning also that you were quite well, which rejoices my heart. And contrary to expectation, my dear, the sun is again shining on us. God bless you, and keep you. Ever yours, affectionately, James Wright. Livelands, 2 o'clock, Jan. 19th."

There had been a fall of snow, and he told her afterwards that he had prayed that their lives "might be as pure as the snow that covered the ground on their wedding day." My dear, good Father! He gave her a Bible that day too, which was the one she ever after used. Is it any wonder that the wedded life of these two was pure and happy, begun as it was with thoughts and prayers so good? It was this Gift of a Bible on her wedding day, that caused Grannie, dear children, to give one to your Mother on her wedding morning. "I had one given to me", she said simply, "I should like Mary to have one too."

The wedding took place in the drawing room, and was of course according to the Episcopal form. Uncle Duthie married them. The hour was 2 o'clock. The brides-maids were Christian Jean Murray, the sister, (always called Jane), and Marion Campbell, afterwards Mrs Forbes, your grand-aunt, dear children. The guests were, Mr and Mrs Murray of Polmaise, Miss Graham of Coldoch, Mr and Miss Brodie, Mr Campbell (your great grandfather, Isobel and Leslie) his three daughters, Anne, Mary, and Marion, his son Robert (your grandfather) and his niece Miss Hasluck; Uncle Mackenzie, Mr Chrystal, Mrs Macnaughton, besides the others already mentioned as being in the house. Mr and Mrs Bruce of Kennet, and Dr and Mrs Pollock (afterwards Pollock-Morris of Craig) and Mr Ramsey of Barnton and Sauchie were invited, but could not come. Miss Margaret Wilsone of Glasgow was also present. She was a niece of the Jacobite Ladies of Murrayshall, and it was she who gave Mother the four beautiful old china plates in the shape of leaves which we now have in the drawing room.

Many jokes had been made to my father about not losing the wedding ring, with a result that he had it so carefully done up in paper that when he had to produce it during the ceremony there was a pause while he took it out of its wrappings!

Mother's dress was white satin. The bridesmaids wore pretty brooches given by the bride and groom, I think the stone is chalcedony, with turquoise forget-me-nots, set in gold. I have the one that was Christian Jane's. Your Mother, dear children, has one, a larger size, which Aunt Duthie wore, and which was also my father's gift. He himself wore a breastpin given to him by his bride, a bird's claw in gold, holding a chrysoprasus. (This was given to your father, my dears, after Grannie's death, in remembrance of her.) After the ceremony, there was wine and cake. Then the bride and bridegroom changed their dresses, had some luncheon, and drove off to Edinburgh in a carriage with four horses. I do not know what Mother's going away dress was, but she wore a satin cloak in an exquisite shade of purple, and a bonnet to match, with ostrich feathers. (I have a "mattress pincushion" made of this cloak, the only bit of it that remains.)

81

Their carriage was the first to drive down the new avenue. Grandmamma writes in her diary, "After the young couple left a little after 4 o'clock we all went to the dining room where we had dinner; went to the drawing room between 7 and 8, and had music, tea and coffee; and after the gentlemen came up, danced till 11 o'clock, when we had supper, songs, and speeches till nearly 1 o'clock, when they separated."

My Grandfather had begun to make the new avenue before Alick's death, but when that sad event happened, he had no heart to go on with it. As soon as Mother's engagement was announced, he determined that she and my father should be the first to drive down it on their wedding day. All hands were set to work at it, and, as Mary Dow told us, they worked with a will, and it was finished just in time. Alas! the old and the new avenues are both away now, and there are houses in their place!

MR WRIGHT'S LETTER TO MR MURRAY

My father and mother went to Gibb's Royal Hotel in Princes Street, Edinburgh, and next day my father wrote this letter to Grandfather:

"My dear Sir, I have the pleasure to inform you that we reached this in safety last night at 20 minutes past seven, having performed the journey in 3 hours and 10 minutes; and I am very happy to say, that my dear Isabella stood the journey very well, and today she is pretty well. We intend to spend the day very quietly, and I have no doubt she will be quite well after another night's sleep. Many a time we wondered last night how you were getting on at Livelands. Mrs Sawer's post boys had no note with them from her, so I did not pay for the horses. I will thank you to pay £1.13.0, not less being the rate I paid at all the others on the road; and I will thank you also to give the stable boy who came out with the carriage yesterday 2/6 on my account, as I came away in such a hurry that I forgot. We have got very good accommodation here, and as the weather is still unsettled, we think of making this our home always at night; and as I have just been told by Isabella that Mr Duthie is to be here on Friday, I have to beg that he takes up his quarters here. With love to all the happy circle at Livelands, and many thanks to Mrs Murray for all her kindness, and hoping soon to have the pleasure of seeing you and Mrs Murray at 225 St Vincent Street, I am, My dear Sir, yours very sincerely, James Wright. Jan. 20th 1841."

GIFTS TO LIVELANDS SERVANTS

My father gave all the house servants at Livelands on the wedding a £1 each; Mary Dow, the lady's maid, £3; and each of the outdoor servants, Gow and Lithgow, the gardeners, Kemp, Littlejohn, Cuthill etc. £1 each. John Freeland was in Edinburgh, and he called on the new married couple the day after their arrival and dined with them; and went with them on Monday to St. Giles where Dr Gordon preached.

They went to their own house in Glasgow on Jan. the 26th, not a very long honey-moon certainly, and were there received by Aunt Jane, who broke shortbread over the bride's head as she crossed the threshold. Aunt Jane left St Vincent Street next day, and went to Calder Park.

MISS MARION CAMPBELL'S LETTER ABOUT THE WEDDING

Mother's bridesmaid, Marion Campbell, wrote to her on Jan. 27th about the wedding:

"As for Papa, I think even yet it is the subject of all others which interests him most. On Wednesday morning he stood with his back to the fire, laughing and joking, and drinking in every word that each of us said with as much enjoyment as if he had been a school boy. I was obliged to go over everything from the time I entered the house in the morning, and found you all laying the cloth, until he was called to say goodbye. And good Mamma, was found sitting up for us in her night cap and dressing gown to hear all about you. She listened with tears in her eyes; dear Isabella, believe me, you have no friend more affectionately interested in you than she is, or more faithful and steady in her regard. I have fairly lost my heart to George (the best man) and almost think the world does not contain another heart like his. We were great allies as you may believe, and everyone said, did our parts to admiration. We all paid our respects at Livelands on Monday, and found the cake much diminished in its fine proportions. They were all in the highest spirits. Jane showed us their gowns, which really are beautiful, and display the good taste of the chooser. I dressed her hair for the dinner at Coldoch, and yesterday she came into me to have another lesson for Polmaise today. Tomorrow she is to come again, and then I think she will be perfect in it for Glasgow. I am very anxious she should be a Belle this season, and make a sensation, which I look forward to her doing, I assure you. Kind regards to Mr Wright. I never saw anyone look so like a bridegroom and a gentleman as he did."

WEDDING CAKE AND PRESENTS

Grandfather highly disapproved of people employing tradesman out of their own towns, he like to give all the custom he could to the Stirling shops, therefore he had the wedding cake made by Scott the confectioner, [90] and it was the first he ever made. Scott and his family carried on business in Stirling for very many years. I think the daughters gave it up not very long before your parent's marriage, dear Isobel and Leslie. Their successors, Keith and Ralston, made your mother's wedding cake, because Grannie wished it to be made in the same shop as her own.

---

90 Alexander Scott established his business at 70 Port Street, Stirling in 1839.

It is now the fashion for everyone who has even a slight acquaintance to a young couple to give them a wedding present, and it has really become quite a tax. Formally, only near relatives or very intimate friends gave presents. Mr Thomas Buchanan gave my Mother the beautiful diamond ring set in blue enamel, (which your mother now possesses). Mrs Murray of Polmaise gave her a large topaz brooch, which I now have. Uncle John gave a beautiful brooch and earrings with long pendants. Part of one of these earrings your mother wears often as a brooch. The four sisters-in-law gave them four large square stools in the drawing room, worked by themselves. Mr Wilson of Carsehill gave my father the large silver tray, with "From J.W. to J.W." inscribed upon it. I believe it is worth now more than £100. (Mother thought so, but we find it is a mistake, 100 ounces of silver is in it).

THE SILVER CLARET JUG

The particularly elegant silver claret jug (now mine), was the gift of Mr William Brown, whose wife was Jane, daughter of Dr Charles Wilsone, a relative of the Jacobite Ladies of Murrayshall. Another daughter of Dr Wilsone's was Mrs Davidson of Ruchill. Mr Brown was an exceedingly gentle, amiable man, and spoke in a mild deprecating way. Some years after my parents' marriage, at a dinner party in St Vincent Street, he said to Mother as he "passed the bottles round" at dessert, "What an exceedingly handsome claret jug, Mrs Wright. I never saw a more elegant shape." "It is indeed," said she, "do you know who gave it to me?" "I have not an idea," said he gently. "It was you," said Mother, rippling over with merriment, and the good man was sorely taken aback, to find he had been praising his own gift.

SILVER KETTLE

The large silver kettle and stand which your Mother now has, was given by George Buchanan, the "best-man." Between him and my father, there was a very strong affection. The silver teapot and quaint old cream pot your Mother uses daily were my father's; and the very handsome, embossed silver tea service that we have in constant use in this house, were bought by him on his marriage. The best tea cups and coffee cups, pink and gold, were also bought by him. Your Mother has the tea cups. They were given to her by Grannie soon after she married. The coffee cups, we have. The dessert service we still use, deep purply-blue with delicately painted flowers, and perforated, embossed borders, was also my father's.[91]

And I may here remark, that his taste was perfect, everything belonging to him was good. And if he said to anyone that her dress was pretty, the wearer was delighted, so well-known was his correct taste. I quite remember our

---

91 These wares were probably from Minton's China Works. The Glasgow Pottery of J & M P Bell & Co made distinctive sets of gold-rimmed pink tea and coffee sets, and painted pierced rim plates similar to those described here, but not before the 1870s.

mother and aunts choosing dresses, and saying, "if James likes them, we may be sure they are right."

FIRST VISITORS AFTER THE MARRIAGE

The house in St Vincent Street was fairly well appointed, and Aunt Jane left it in perfect order, so Mother was able to have visitors at once. The first were Uncle and Aunt Duthie and Aunt Jane Murray, they arrived on the 29th of January. The two former returned to England. Aunt Jane Murray paid a long visit. On Saturday, March 27th, Grandmamma writes in her diary that she and Grandpapa went by the 12 o'clock stage coach to Glasgow, where my father met them with with a "noddy",

"Arrived at 3 o'clock, and found Isabella and Jane quite well. Old Mr and Mrs Buchanan dined with us. On Sunday went to St David's Church, the minister Mr Lorimer (afterwards Dr Lorimer)[92] and in the afternoon to St Jude's (Episcopal Church) incumbent, Mr Montgomerie.[93] Monday, a dinner party of twenty.

Tuesday, 30th, all went an excursion, left Glasgow at 8am., by railroad to Irvine, where they found Dr Pollok's carriage waiting to take Mother to Cunninghamhead House. (The Polloks lived there then, it was before Dr Pollok succeeded to Craig, dropped the "Dr" and became Mr Pollok-Morris.) The rest of the party went on to Ayr, drove to Burns' Monument etc., and returned by rail to Irvine, picked up Mother, and got back to Glasgow at 4 o'clock, and all dined that evening at Uncle and Aunt John's, a party of 20. There was another dinner party at Mr Davidson's, Ruchill,[94] and another at Mr Young's in Blythswood Square;[95] and after all this gaiety the Livelands party went home on Saturday, April 3rd. There was also, before they left, a dinner party for them at Dowanhill.

FIRST DAYS OF HOUSEKEEPING

As I said, dear Aunt Jane left the house in perfect order for the young wife, but her servants had not been very satisfactory. Possibly she could not dismiss them and get others, monthly engagements being unknown then, so she bound them over to behave well to the young mistress, and this they promised. But she ought to have warned Mother about their shortcomings. She, however, contented herself with giving Mother minute directions about locking the larder door, after giving out all that was wanted for dinner

---

92 John Gordon Lorimer was Minister of St David's (Ramshorn), Ingram Street.

93 R Montgomery was Minister of St Jude's Episcopal Chapel in Blythswood Square.

94 James Davidson, Merchant, bought Ruchill House (built 1700, now within Ruchill Hospital) in 1835 and made some additions to it.

95 George Young, 8 Blythswood Square, of G & R Young and Co, Merchants.

or breakfast, all which directions Mother duly followed. But she had had little-housekeeping experience, and was accustomed to the comfortable servants at Livelands, where everything moved smoothly under Grandmamma's wise rule. The maids soon took advantage of her inexperience, and things came to a crisis, when a preposterous account came in for filling the kitchen spice-box. Mother told me laughing, once when I was taking some spices out of it, that is always made her think of how her eyes were opened to the iniquities of her maids. They were then dismissed, and Mother wrote to Grandmama to send her good servants from Stirling; and then began, at the May term, 1842, the good luck which is still ours in possessing good maids. I said "good luck", but I like to record it as one of the "many mercies" for which I desire to be grateful.

JENNY FINLAYSON AND JENNY WELSH, MAY 1842

Jenny Finlayson, (Jenny Finlayson got £6.10.0 in the half year. Jenny Welsh £5.1.0. Out of this they took their own tea and sugar. These were thought good wages then.) was the cook, and only left after 14 years because of old age. Jenny Welsh was housemaid, remained with us through all sorrows and money trials, accommodating herself to changed circumstances with loving cheerfulness and only leaving us, Feb. 14. 1883, from latter inability to work any longer for us she held so dear. She died on Sunday, August 27th 1893. She is buried in the old churchyard of St Ninians. Old John Brown told me with tears in his eyes, "I had the pleesure of laying her heid in the grave." Your father, my dears, kindly went to her funeral and took the feet.

And when I hear the old church bell toiling on Sunday mornings, after the modern bells in Stirling have done clanging, I think of Jenny lying restfully there, dear Jenny, good and faithful servant, I hope sometimes, somewhere, I shall hear your kindly voice say "you're my own child, my dear Miss Isabella", just as you so often did! I may here say, the inscription on the old bell of St Ninians is:

> *"Such wondrous power to Musicke's given,*
> *It elevates the soul to heaven."*

JENNY WELSH AND MENIE MACKENZIE

The two Jennys left Stirling by stagecoach, and on arriving at Castlecary,[96] found the railway was opened from there to Glasgow, and the train was to go for the first time, so they got into a truck, enterprising Jennys, and arrived safely, and very much pleased with this exploit. Jenny Welsh, of course, knew Mother well, having been in Bishop Gleig's service for seven years, and it must have been an immense comfort to Mother to have a "kent" face about her, as she was then in a delicate state of health.

---

96   Castlecary is 6 miles east south east of Falkirk and was the junction of the Caledonian and Scottish Central Railway lines.

Before long Mrs Mackenzie, Menie, arrived, and at one o'clock on Wednesday June 22nd 1842 Jane Ann was born. Jenny said, "We were just going to our dinner when we heard Mrs Wright had got a daughter and there was great rejoicing in the kitchen, and I ate a capital dinner after hearing the news."

Dear Mother was very ill. Aunt Eliza was staying in the house, and Mrs Pollock Morris too. When the latter came, poor Mother whispered, "Janet, you've just come to see me die." My father was greatly delighted with his baby. "With what pleasure I shall take her by the hand, and lead her through the streets", said he exultingly to Aunt Eliza. "It's a pity it was not a boy," said someone to him, "I am delighted with my daughter," said he, beaming. Neither he nor Mother cared whether they had boys or girls, "We get what is best for us," said he; and I have often heard her say that she was thankful when she found her babies were "like other people", and cared nothing for the sex. "But", said she to me, years after, when your Mother, my dears, was married, "though I never particularly wanted a son, it's very nice now that I have one"! And indeed your father was a good and kind son to her. That, too, was one of the "many mercies."

MR BUCHANAN ON THE BIRTH OF "WEE JEAN"

On hearing of the baby's arrival, old Mr Buchanan of Dowanhill wrote this note to my father:

"Dowanhill, Thursday Morning, June 23rd 1842. My dear Sir, I congratulate you on the birth of wee Jean, and pray and trust that she may be spared to be a Blessing to you and her mother. This event brings to my recollection the birth of another wee Jean, on a morning in August 1783, when we were preparing to attend a Race at Hamilton. Offer my affectionate regards to Mrs Wright, and my sincere good wishes that all may go well with herself and her important charge. Dear Sir, yours truly, James Buchanan."

You will see by this mention of the day-old baby as "wee Jean" that it never entered into the old man's mind that there could be any departure from the old Scottish custom of naming the first girl after the mother's mother. The wee Jean of whose birth in 1783 he speaks, was, of course, his ward, Jean Buchanan of Croy, the baby's grandmother. It was July 29th she was born, not August.

There was a large party at 225 St Vincent Street for the christening which took place on Tuesday, soon after 5 o'clock, Grandpapa and Grandmamma from Livelands, Uncle and Aunt Duthie, Jane and Margaret Duthie, Aunt Jane Murray, Uncle Munro and Aunt Agnes, Aunts Jane, Margaret and Eliza from Calder Park, Uncle John and his sister-in-law Miss Fanny Logan, John Freeland, Mr James Wilson of Carsehill, Mr and Mrs Buchanan of Dowanhill, Mr Tom Buchanan, Dr Hannay, and Dr Lorimer of St David's, who officiated.

The baby received the name of Jane Anne. Jane for her own Grandmother (Jean was then unfashionable) Anne for her stepgrandmother, and because of the latter the double name continued to be used out of compliment to her. Very much pleased good Grandmamma was at this attention on Mother's part. She had felt hurt when Aunt Duthie called her fourth daughter Charlotte, and not Anne; and she showed her pleasure very substantially by leaving Jane Anne in her will a large supply of silver and linen.

The robe in which the baby was dressed was used by us all at our christenings. You wore it too, my dear children, when you were christened, and your Mother has it now, carefully put away for her grandchildren in years to come. Uncle Duthie gave the baby an embossed, silver mug, and Grandmamma gave her a silver fork, knife, and spoon. (Auntie Jean gave you, Leslie, the fork, knife, and spoon, when you were christened, as you are her god-child). After the ceremony, Mother, Jane and Margaret Duthie retired, the other twenty dined at 6 o'clock. Father, Mother, Baby and Aunt Eliza, with old Menie Mackenzie the nurse, went to Livelands on the 23rd of July; and on the 10th of August, they all drove to Coldoch to lunch, Baby too! Dear Mother was very happy. Aunt Eliza told me she never saw anyone carry a baby as gracefully as she did. She had a beautiful figure, sloping shoulders, and a head well poised, and looked every inch a lady.

MY FATHER AT THE LEVÉE IN DALKEITH PALACE
SEPTEMBER 5TH 1842

The Queen and Prince Albert arrived at Granton, September 1st 1842, and took up their abode at Dalkeith Palace. There were splendid illuminations on the 2nd in Edinburgh in their honour. Grandpapa, Grandmamma, Aunt Jane Murray, Uncle and Miss Mackenzie, and my father were staying in Edinburgh, and enjoyed the sight very much. On Saturday the 3rd they were all in a window in Queensferry Street, and saw the Royal Procession pass on its way from the Castle to Dalmeny Park.

The Queen held a Levée at Dalkeith Palace on the 5th, and my father was presented by Henry Dundas of Craigton, Lord Provost of Glasgow. My father was then Treasurer of the City of Glasgow, an office which he held six years. He was asked to head a deputation to her Majesty, and had he accepted, would have been knighted, but he found out that another man was dying for the honour. I think this man was Andrew Orr, a stationer or some such thing, who as Sir Andrew bought Harvieston Castle[97] at the foot of the Ochils, the home of Dr Tait, Archbishop of Canterbury. We have my father's court dress, and I remember his dressing up in it for our amusement when we were children. The sword, he borrowed from a friend.

97 Harvieston Castle, between Dollar and Tillicoultry was burned down in 1970 and demolished 1973.

The Bow, Stirling. Watercolour Sketch by Jane Anne Wright. Smith Art Gallery And Museum

When the Queen signified her intention of visiting Stirling Castle, there was some difficulty about finding anyone capable of driving a four-in-hand up and down the steep streets. At last Mr Ramsay,[98] a noted horseman, laird of Barnton and Sauchie, agreed to do so, and Grandpapa, his great friend, and as good in the management of horses as he, promised to sit by him on the box. They drove up and down to the Castle several times in preparation, but it was easy enough when there were no crowds. The ticklish part was in the Bow, (alas! now called Bow Street!) where the leaders at the sharp corner, were of course out of sight of the driver. It was safely accomplished when the Royal party came on Tuesday the 13th and the Queen could not have had a safer driver than Ramsay of Barnton; but she did not know that, poor young thing, and the cheering and firing were trying for the horses, order was not very well kept, and it is said she had tears of fright in her pretty eyes.

After it was over, Mr Ramsay confessed to Grandpapa that he was truly thankful when he got them safe down about 12 o'clock. The Queen and Prince then drove to Hopetoun, and the Livelands party went to the Stamp Office[99] to see them pass, all but Grandpapa, who had been obliged to forego the pleasure of sitting on the box of the Queen's coach, having caught a chill which ended in inflammation of the liver. According to the heroic treatments of the times, he was bled in the arm and had twenty-four leeches on as well. Surely in those days, it was the survival of the fittest!

STOPPING THE ROYAL PROCESSION. "EASY IN FRONT THERE!"

He had sufficiently recovered on the 13th, to go down to the gate of Livelands Avenue to watch the Royal Procession pass on its way to Hopetoun. When he arrived at the gate, he saw a number of people standing outside. The ground inside the gate sloped up to the wall above the road, and the genial old man at once invited everyone in so as to have a better view. They soon saw the royal carriage in coming along, proceeded by a mounted guard, going at a handsome trot. Grandpapa knew there was no chance of getting a good view of the Queen at the pace they were going, and quick as thought he determined to have it. Were his loyal, old eyes to be cheated of the sight he had come to see, surgeon, lancet, and twenty four leeches not withstanding! By no means! So, as the guard approached, in a loud voice the old cavalry officer shouted, "Easy in front there!" Of course the soldiers at the word of command, instantly drew in their horses, and the whole procession passed at a walking pace, Grandpapa, and everyone near him having a splendid view.

98   William Ramsay of Barnton (1809-1850) MP for Stirling was well known in racing and hunting circles throughout Scotland and was chief promoter of the Stirling Races in King's Park.

99   The Stamp Office was then at 56 King Street.

O dear old Grandpapa! I think I see you now, your straight figure, aristocratic bearing, thick white hair, and bright blue eyes! How genial and merry, and hearty you were! How you would roar with laughter at the success of your plan! My father used to tell a story of it with much amusement.

You see, dear children, you come of rather audacious "forebears", your great great grandfather William Wilson was accessory to the throwing of the future King George the Fourth out of a window; and your great grandfather John Murray caused Queen Victoria to pass slowly before him, that he might see her well! And as to your grandfather James Wright, I have told the story of his calmly working his way close to the Queen's side, that he might pray God's blessing on her fair, young head. (Your great, great, great grandfather John Wordie of Cambusbarron, refreshed Prince Charlie with cake and wine near where the schoolhouse at Cambusbarron now stands).

ILLNESS OF CHRISTIAN JANE MURRAY

I have been recounting all kinds of sorts of cheerful things, but in the end of 1842, sorrow came to Livelands, in the illness of Aunt Jane Murray. Very dear was this child to her father, the baby who was christened on her mother's funeral day. Dear beyond words to her stepmother, who brought her up with such loving care that the child never even found out that she was not her own mother till she was seven years old. Then she startled and grieved her, naughty little puss, by addressing her as Mrs Murray. "It was the only time", said poor Grandmama to Mary Dow, "that I ever felt inclined to give her a whipping."

Corporal punishment was considered by most people absolutely necessary in those days to the successful training of the young. "If you spare the rod, you spoil the child" was the firm belief of many parents and guardians. But certainly little Jane got no "whippings", and led a very happy life at Livelands, her only regret being that she was not a boy, so that she might always go about the fields with her father, among the "stots"[100] she was so fond of, "instead of learning to play the piano." She and Mary Dow, and her old dog Rover, used to take a basket of eatables, and spend hours in the grounds. Rover died, and was succeeded by a puppy, called Pincher in the summer of 1840. I remember dear Pincher in his old age.

Jane paid several visits to St Vincent Street after Mother's marriage, and a strong mutual affection grew up between her and my father. As to Aunt Eliza, long years after the young girl's death, she spoke of her with emotion, as "the most perfect Christian character" she had known.

100 Young bullocks.

In November 1842, Mother went to Livelands with Jane Anne and Menie, and Jane went one day to meet my father. There had been a heavy fall of snow that day, the 25th, and she got her feet wet, and never seemed quite well afterwards. No doubt it only wanted some such thing to develop the chest delicacy that she probably inherited from her mother. In January, 1843, she had influenza, and my father went to see her, and returned to Glasgow saying he thought her very ill. On the 27th, Mother had a little note from her, "They say I am better, but do not believe them, Isabella." Mother exclaimed, "I must go at once, I am sure her case is not understood," and with my father went that day to Livelands. When they arrived there, Mother was told that as Jane was feverish it would not be wise to go into the room, as Mother was nursing her baby. But nothing ever could keep Mother from anyone she loved. Upstairs she went to the nursery, and poor Jane knew her, and was pleased, but of course she had to go back to Glasgow that day.

Dr Johnston (father of the present doctor 1895) had taken Dr Wordie to see her in consultation, but my father was not satisfied, and took Dr Hannay, his own doctor in Glasgow, to see her on Feb. 6th. On the 10th, he and Mother went to Livelands to stay, for the end seemed near. Jane was quite happy. She asked to see all the servants, "and spoke beautifully to them", said faithful Mary Dow. At 20 minutes past 12, on Wed. Feb. 15th she died. She was in her twentieth year. She was laid to rest in the Polmaise vault in the old Churchyard, St Ninians, Mr Henderson officiating, on Tuesday the 21st at 2 o'clock. And her death left Livelands very desolate indeed.

MARY DOW, LADY'S MAID

Mary Dow stayed on in attendance on Grandmamma till Nov. 1845, when she left after being there thirteen years. In her old age, she lived in Linlithgow, and used to come to see us every summer, and delight us with her reminiscences. "I often wonder, Mrs Wright, what you feel when you think of Mr Henderson," said she with the easy frankness of a privileged old servant. "Tut, Mary," said Mother, "I often wonder what you feel when you think of Lithgow." Lithgow was one of the Liveland's servants, and an admirer of Mary's. When she died, it was found that she had left all her little savings to Mother. She had relations, but had never cared for them. Mother, however, sent for them, and divided the money between them. The little pearl ring always worn by Aunt Jane Murray, was given to Aunt Eliza who wore it in remembrance of her. She, in turn, gave it to Jane Anne. Her Bible, bound in red morocco, Mother kept, and as soon as I could read she gave it to me. I have the little Bible still.

"THREE CRAWS SAT ON A STANE"

After her death, Grandpapa and Grandmamma went in April to St Vincent Street, they were very sorrowful, poor dear people. My father took them to

Calder Park one day. Aunt Eliza was also at St Vincent Street, and grew more and more attached to Grandmamma. Grandpapa was very fond of his little granddaughter. He liked her being named after his two wives, but he often spoke of her as "Jean." He used to sing a little song to amuse her.

> *"Three craws sat upon a stane,*
> *Ane flew awa', and then there were twa.*
> *Twa craws sat on a stane,*
> *Ane flew awa', and then there was ane.*
> *Ane craw sat on a stane,*
> *He flew awa' and then there was nane!"*

The flying awa' of the craw was acted by fluttering both hands. No doubt "Old Isobel" crooned this little song when her baby son sat on her knee in the old house at Torbrex.

ISABELLA MACKENZIE

At the May Term 1843, Isabella Murray Mackenzie came to Glasgow as Jane Anne's nurse. She was Menie Mackenzie's daughter, and was named after my Mother. After being nurse for about a year or more, Nurse Margaret came, and she then became table maid. She had been in the service of your grandmother, Mrs Campbell, dear Isabel and Leslie, but had always meant to go to her "own young lady" as soon as she got the chance. Your grandmother was not over well pleased at her leaving her, as she was a good servant.

IGIE

She was known to us children by no other name than Igie, which was the name given to her by Jane Anne as soon as she began to speak. She was tall, with fine eyes, dark hair, and clear skin "even the minister (Doctor Sommerville) called her 'Mrs Wright's handsome table maid'", said Jenny. She left us to marry John Stewart. We still keep up communication with her children and grandchildren; one little granddaughter bears the name of Murray Wright, so called by her mother Mrs McNeil in compliment to the two families, although among her little flock, she already had a Mary and an Isabella.

Menie left when her daughter Isabella came. It was a long time, a year, to keep a monthly nurse, but naturally Mother felt her baby was sure to be well cared for by her, who had been so long associated with the Murray family, and loved them as her own.

VISIT TO STANLEY HOUSE, PERTHSHIRE

In June of that year the family went to stay at Livelands, and Grandmamma writes in her journal that on the 30th she, my father, mother, baby, and Igie drove from Livelands all the way to Auchterarder where the Buchanans' carriage met them, and took them to Stanley. A fire was lit in the room where Igie and the baby were to sleep, and the chimney promptly took fire, which was not surprising as it had been stuffed with a bag of straw, and whoever lit the fire forgot it was there. It was speedily put out, and the house escaped for that time; but a few years ago it was burned down. Grandpapa joined the party, by way of Perth. They all called one day at Meikleour, where Mr and Mrs John Murray then lived. He succeeded to Polmaise, and was father of the present Laird, Colonel John Murray (1895). A pleasant week was spent at Stanley.

ARDROSSAN

September was spent at Ardrossan by my parents and Jane Anne, and in a house two doors off, Grandmamma and the aunts from Calder Park lodged. The grandparents from Livelands and Mrs Alick Macgregor came to stay with our parents, and my kindly father took the whole party an expedition to Arran, where they dined at Lamlash, and saw the arrival of the Marquis of Douglas and his bride at Brodick.

BIRTH OF MARGARET WILSONE WRIGHT, 1844

On Saturday, Oct. 5th 1844, at 9.30am another little girl was born; and on Thursday Nov. 7th there was a large party for her christening, 23 in all, Grandpapa and Grandmamma from Livelands, Dr and Mrs Hannay, Miss Logan, Mr and Mrs James Buchanan, George and Tom Buchanan, Mr and Mrs James Freeland from America, John Freeland, Mr and Mrs John Wright, Mr and Mrs Munro from Rutherglen and their little girl Maggie, Aunts Jane, Margaret and Eliza, and Dr Lorimer, the Minister.

CHRISTENING OF MARGARET WILSONE WRIGHT. NURSE MARGARET

The little one was christened between 4 and 5, and received the name of Margaret Wilsone, after Grandmama at Calder Park. Mother always spelt the Wilsone with an 'e'; she liked it because of her old relations, the Jacobite Ladies of Murrayshall. The dinner hour was 6 o'clock.

Mother was not able to nurse this baby, and it was then that Jenny Welsh told her about Margaret Henderson from Stirling. Nurse Margaret, who soon came, leaving her own little child Louisa in her mother's care. After some time, her sister Mary brought the child from Stirling to Glasgow (where she was born) and she was christened in our house. Mother knew about Mrs Henderson, the mother, a widow with a large family, who supported herself by cleaning and turning straw bonnets, a great industry in those days,[101] unknown now, and often went with Jenny Macnab to give her orders. She lived then in Broad Street, but in our time in a very old house in The Bow, up a dark and winding stair.

Maggie, the new baby, was a very lovely child, and Nurse Margaret used to come in from her walks radiant with delight at the remarks made on her beauty. She was often stopped by people asking "whose is that beautiful child"? Some grieved her by saying she was too pretty to live; and one croaking, would be prophetess roused her to violent wrath by affirming that no child every lived long, who had a delicate blue vein such as Maggie had somewhere on the "bridge" of her baby nose. Poor dear Nurse Margaret, she lavished on her foster child the love that ought to have been bestowed on her own little baby. I believe Nurse Margaret was twenty-one when she became Nurse in St Vincent Street. Never were babies more spotlessly clean, never were nurseries more daintily kept, and she spared no pains to train us all in the way that we should go.

DINNER PARTY AT THE BANK OF SCOTLAND, STIRLING

In the little diary written by Grandmamma at Livelands, I find one or two notes of the year before Maggie's birth, which I shall enter before writing further. On July 28th, 1843, she records that she and Grandpapa, and our parents went to Mr Brodie's, The Bank of Scotland House,[102] Stirling, to the christening of his grandchild, Louisa Maclaverty. (His daughter, Annie Brodie, was the wife of Mr MacLaverty of Kiel in Argyllshire.) Mr Henderson, Episcopal clergyman, christened the child, and there was a large dinner party afterwards, among the guests being Miss Mary and Miss Grace Speirs of Laurel Hill, aunts of Harriet and Anna who now own the place (1895). My father took Miss Grace into dinner, and years afterwards she told Jane Anne how much she had "enjoyed his company" "I felt, my dear," said she, "that I was beside a good man." She said that he and she sat on the side of the dinner table facing the windows. You will think I am degenerating into twaddle, dear children, but I thought you might like to know just where he sat. How little he suspected that you, his only grandchildren would be born in that very house!

THE NOBLEMEN, BURIED UNDER THE PRESENT BANK OF SCOTLAND, STIRLING

And indeed, the site where it stands is of peculiar interest to us; because there, before the high altar of the church of the Dominican Monastery [103]

---

101 A bill survives in the McCutcheon Stirling Collection, issued by Mrs Muir, Millinery and Straw Bonnet Rooms, King Street, Stirling, for the cleaning, lining, alteration and addition of tulle to a bonnet in 1853 at a cost of 3/1d.

102 Baker Street/Friar Street, built in 1834; architect William Burn, and still extant. Mr Brodie was the Bank of Scotland agent in Stirling 1833-1863.

103 The Black Friars or Dominicans came to Stirling c1233. Recent excavation has shown that the Black Friars Church is now under Murray Place, near the main Post Office. See *Proceedings of the Society of Antiquaries of Scotland* 126 (1996) 881-898.

which stood there, and which gave the name Friars'Wynd (now, disgraceful! Friars' Street!) to the road running past it, were buried the bodies of the old Earl of Lennox, his son-in-law Murdoch, Duke of Albany, with the two sons of the latter. From this Earl of Lennox, and Duke of Albany, we claim descent, through the Haldanes of Lanrick. Miss Grace Speirs also told Jane Anne that a relative of hers, in days gone by, had married a Mr Wright. This, no doubt, was the mother of William (or James?) Wright my great grandfather.

DEATH OF ANNE, MRS MURRAY OF POLMAISE

On Dec. 14th, 1843, died Mrs Murray of Polmaise. Grandmamma writes that there were nearly 100 people at her funeral. She was Anne Maxwell of Monreith, and had three aunts duchesses. She and her husband were generally known as "William and Anne." She was greatly beloved by all ranks, a queenly woman, I have heard Mother say. She was looked upon as the Queen of the County. She had no children, but this did not prevent her taking to her heart the children of her husband's cousin and many happy days Mother spent at Polmaise (now of course Old Polmaise). Mother showed me the room that was Mrs Murray's boudoir, and where she, as a little girl, used to like to go when the housekeeper was getting the orders. A good deal of state was kept up at Polmaise in those days, a piper played the guests into dinner, and the servants wore light blue liveries. It was Lady Agnes Murray, first wife of the present laird (1895) who changed the light blue liveries, for very dark blue, nearly black.

DEATH OF MRS KEITH

Another entry in Grandmamma's diary is,

"Dear Aunt Keith died on Monday, March 3rd 1845, and was buried in the Balhadie Aisle, Dunblane Cathedral on Sat. 8th. Eight gentlemen came from Edinburgh (she died in 9 Forth Street) with the hearse, amongst them Mr Biggs, her priest. Mr Murray dined with them at the Royal Hotel on returning from Dunblane."

There was at Livelands, an oil painting in the drawing room of "dear Aunt Keith", but I never loved to gaze upon her as I did upon sweet Mrs MacGregor. Mrs Keith was attired in her portrait in such scanty garments, that we children always called her "the naked lady." This picture, when Grandpapa left Livelands, was sent to some of her relatives. He only had it for his life-time, and Mother advised him to send it off then, rather than remove it to Melville Place. "Aunt Keith" was a Roman Catholic.

The quaint silver salt spoon in the shape of a spade which Mother gave to me, has a K. on it. It either belonged to "Aunt Keith" or to Grandmama's cousin, Mrs Keith of Dunottar and Ravelston who died at Cleveden in 1847. She was Margaret Oliphant of Gask, sister of the sweet Scottish song-writer,

Caroline, Baroness Nairne. Ravelston, near Edinburgh, was long in the possession of the Keiths. It was Keith of Ravelston, Andrew by name, who was one of the few to escape alive from the bloody field of Flodden. He was, I think, the one who carried the news of that terrible defeat to Edinburgh, or else he was Provost of the town at that time. I am not quite sure which. Ravelston was sold and is now in the possession of Miss Murray Gartshare (1895).

AT GOUROCK IN 1846

The summer of 1846 was spent by my parents and their two children in Mileburn Cottage, Gourock, and there as usual they had their relatives, of both families, to visit them, and made many pleasant excursions together. It was at Gourock that Jenny Welsh was nearly struck by lightning. My father and Aunt Eliza were on their way home from church in a terrific thunderstorm. They saw Jenny some distance before them, and near the gate of the house, a blinding flash of lightning caused her to stagger. Aunt Eliza exclaimed, "Jenny is struck", (she told us she heard our father at the same moment half in a whisper say, "vain is the help of man"!) And they hurried after her. She managed to totter into the house, where she fainted.

BIRTH OF ISABELLA MURRAY WRIGHT, 1846

In the end of August, 1846, Mother and the two children and nurses went to Calder Park. Another baby was expected in about two months time. Mother was walking with grandmamma and the aunts in the high field above the house when she became ill, and at once declared that she must go home to Glasgow. The village doctor, Dr Orr, was summoned and said she must remain where she was, but poor Mother could not be pacified, and pined for home. So the car was got, and she set off with Aunt Margaret, and Nurse Mary, and Dr Orr in attendance. In the village, they met my father, calmly walking up the hill to Calder Park, and he returned at once and went with them. At every station the train stopped at, old Dr Orr begged Mother to get out. But they arrived safely at St Vincent Street, where they found all the carpets up and Jenny having a great cleaning. The journey was a most terrible risk, and dear Mother continued ill for two days, certainly, (I rather think three) and then Sept. 3rd twins were born, one, a boy, dead, the other a poor little mite of a girl, (myself!) who would possibly not have survived long had it not been for Aunt Margaret's persistent rubbings with whisky to keep up the feeble circulation.

Dr Rainy, our own dear doctor, was away for a holiday, meaning to be back long before the event was expected, so Dr Orr remained with Mother till his return; this, however, greatly to Dr Orr's delight, was not till after I was born; and the good man went back to Lochwinnoch with such a big fee in his pocket from my grateful and exultant father, that he announced that he wouldn't mind if Mrs Wright had a baby every month, if he were with her as doctor. Mother told me that when Menie took me to her to look at, she said, "This shall be my own daughter." She spoke of this in one of our last conversations, just before her death. When I was a very young child, she must have said it to me, because when I could barely know what "daughter" meant, I use to say when I wanted to be petted, "I'm your daughter, am I not, Mama?", and she invariably said "Yes my own daughter."

Grandmamma at Livelands, the faithful chronicler of family events, was ill at this time, so there is a long gap in her little diary, which I have no means of filling up. But I know I was christened by Dr Lorimer and received my Mother's name. By the way, the beautiful china bowl used at all our christenings, and bought by my father for that purpose, is still in our drawing room.

THE NEW NURSERIES

New nurseries had been built by my father after Maggie's birth, comfortable sunny rooms at the top of the house, with a pleasant view across fields to the Clyde. Houses were soon built in every part, but as our house stood high, the row of houses immediately behind did not shut out the sunshine. They were the only rooms on that floor, and had every convenience. There were no self filling boilers in those days, but the nursery fire was provided with a large boiler which had to be kept constantly filled. There were plenty of cupboards, a sink, and even a large "bunker" for coals in the big closet where the pots and pans, etc., were kept. So we were quite "self-contained."

To these comfortable nurseries, Nurse Margaret's tender care to bring me up "by hand" (Mother tried to nurse me but could not) and to my sister Maggie's passionate love, I was relegated as soon as Menie left. But I was a poor, feeble, little thing, Glasgow air did not suit me, or rather perhaps it had not the chance, because I screamed wildly every time I was taken out, which may have been fear of the street noises, but Doctor Rainy declared it was the air, so Nurse Margaret, Maggie and I spent a good deal of our time at Livelands or Calder Park till I grew stronger.

On Sept. 24th, 1846, the Livelands grandparents were returning from Balhadie, when the horse fell, and they were both much bruised and shaken, though no bones were broken. On Nov. 26th Grandmamma became ill and was not able to leave her room until Feb., 1847. Jeannie Kemp had succeeded Mary Dow as her maid. She was the daughter of Kemp, the overseer at the farm of Braehead, on which farm Grandpapa spent most money, no doubt, but farming was a great delight to him. Kemp died, but with his usual kindness, Grandpapa let the widow, her 2 daughters and 4 sons, stay on at Braehead in the upper floor of the farmhouse. Margaret, the eldest, came to St Vincent Street, as under-nurse, but had to leave, as she was subject to epileptic fits. Poor things, there was insanity in the family, and two of the sons in after years were temporally deranged. While Grandmamma was so ill, the faithful Menie, Mrs Mackenzie went to Livelands, and stayed some months, helping Jeannie Kemp to nurse her.

The summer of 1847 was spent by us at Gourock. This time, the larger family had to go to Mileburn House instead of as before to Mileburn Cottage. You see a baby, though ever so small, takes up a great deal of room. The grandparents from Livilands paid a visit there, and William Wright came home there from Australia in June. The Duthie's were among the other visitors, and with pretty Margaret Duthie, then about 15 or 16, William promptly fell in love. He returned to Australia without proposing to her, she being so very young; but though he married in after years, I know from Aunt Eliza and others that she was the love of his life, indeed his own son (Willie) said so to me not very long ago. Grandmama, being better, resumes her diary, and says that on hearing from her that Mrs Wright had a third daughter, Mr Chrystal, writer in Stirling, who liked to make a joke, remarked "now Mrs Wright has the Three Graces"!

MAGGIE IS LOST AT GOUROCK 1847

There was a great alarm at Mileburn House on one Sunday. Nearly everyone was at Church, and Maggie toddled out to the garden alone. She had a little parasol, pretty dear, and was seen to put it up, and trot about, she was so proud of her parasol. But when someone called to her to come in, she was nowhere to be found. Nurse Margaret came home from Church, and was quite beside herself with misery. Poor Mother's first thought was, that she had gone down to the rocky shore, and fallen in. Her next, that the gypsies had stolen her. Gypsies often, even when I remember Gourock later, frequented some caves on the hill-side, and they had been seen there the day before. Little children were sometimes stolen then, for the sake of their clothes and good looks. But Maggie was found safe in a little toll bar, that I remember well, a little wooden box, just like a Punch and Judy show, kept by an old man and his daughter Mary. The old man saw Maggie go past holding up her little parasol, and sent Mary after her. They did not know to whom she belonged, so kept her in the little toll bar till some of her "ain folk" came along, making anxious enquiries. She was not a bit frightened, and was found quite good and happy beside the old man and his daughter.

DEATH OF MRS MURRAY OF LIVELANDS 1848

On the 12th of Sept., 1847, William Murray of Polmaise, died, and was succeeded by his cousin John Murray, whose wife Elizabeth Bryce was daughter of a doctor in Edinburgh. They were the parents of the present Laird (1895). The last notice in Grandmamma's diary is on Christmas Day 1847, "Mr and Miss Chrystal, Uncle Mackenzie and Dr Johnston (father of the present doctor 1895) dined here. I was too ill to go downstairs, but stayed in the drawing room." She died April the 5th 1848. Her death left dear Grandpapa very desolate. He was always so good and brave about his bereavement, but when he came back from her funeral in the old churchyard, Mother said he lent his stately old head on the drawing room mantlepiece, and wept. (Jane Anne was at Livelands for the funeral.)

Her brother, Donald Macgregor, Laird of Balhadie, was weakly in intellect and in body too. He would never go away from his own lands, because he imagined that if he did, he would no longer be the Laird. Had he died before his sister, she would have succeeded him. As this might have been the case Grandmamma wrote in her will, that she left Balhadie to Grandpapa and after him to Alick, failing him to Jane. This was quite nice and natural for her to do, these two, from becoming her charges so young, being like her own children. Failing Jane it was to go to Aunt Duthie and Mother.

She left all her possessions to her husband's family, jewels, books, pictures. Of the latter, one, "dear Aunt Keith's", was only Grandpapa's for life. The miniatures of Prince Charlie and the Cardinal of York given to her ancestor, and also the lock of Prince Charlie's hair are now in the possession of the Duthies at Row. The beautiful aquamarine brooch given to her by Lord Nairne when she married, I often wear. Among the Jacobite relics, is the ring in memory of the brother of Sir Ewan Cameron of Locheil. This brother was the last Jacobite who was executed for his adherence to the Stuarts. The ring bears the inscription "Dina Forget." (It is in Grannie's Jewel Box, dear children). To Jane Anne to whom she was much attached, she left her watch, linen, and silver. The little old musical snuff box which has so often delighted you, Isobel and Leslie, as well as your aunts and mother in childhood days, was Grandmamma's, and she often made it play for Jane Anne's amusement. She made a rag doll for her, painted its face, and dressed it in green silk. It was called Meg Merrilees. It was the remembrance of the pleasure of this doll, which we still have gave, to Jane Anne that caused her to make one for you, Isobel. Both you and Leslie lavished affection on "Betty Campbell"!

Among Grandmamma's things were some beautiful albums. We have ten of them. It was the fashion then to keep an album, and to get one's friends to write or paint something in them. Grandmamma's friends must certainly have been clever, for many of the pictures are exceedingly well done.

My father, at Grandpapa's request, became a Burgess of Stirling. His Burgess ticket is dated June 3rd, 1848. His burgess ticket of Glasgow is dated August 29th, 1829. About this time, the beautiful portrait in oils of my grandmother at Calder Park was painted. My father engaged an artist to paint the likeness of his mother, a Mr Carr, and he spent three weeks in the village of Lochwinnoch to do so. When it was finished, it was propped up against something in the Calder Park drawing room before being hung up; and I toddled into the drawing room, and gazed in surprise at it and then at Grandmamma, "O, two Grandmammas!" said I, and was kissed and hugged by all the aunts for my unconscious appreciation of the likeness.

Mr Carr also painted the portraits of Jane Anne, Maggie and myself, which hang now in our dining room. I was originally painted with a big doll, but it was taken out, because it looked so like another baby. The little basket in Jane Ann's hand, we still have. Truly we are a conservative family!

THE DISRUPTION IN 1843

From the time of the Disruption, 1843, my father had connected himself with the Free Church. I think there is now a feeling that the Disruption was a mistake, and might have been averted. I do not know enough about the matter to form an opinion, but I think so great a split was sad; I do, however, very highly honour the men who for conscience sake, "came out" at that time, leaving churches, manses, glebes, stipends uncomplainingly; and bravely bearing many discomforts, not only for themselves, but for their wives and families. Because, remember, it was for conscience sake. Many great and learned men left the Church of Scotland then, the greatest, I suppose, being Dr Chalmers to whom my father was much attached.

The sad part of the Disruption, was the exceedingly bitter feeling that existed between the two parties, so bitter that is seems almost ludicrous to recall some of the incidents. I quite remember Aunt Jane pegging along the hot and dusty six miles between Innerwick Free Church Manse and Dunbar one scorching summer day, hurrying too, to be in time to see us off by train from Dunbar. "I hoped some carriage would have overtaken you, and picked you up, Jane" said Mother, distressed at seeing her so hot and tired. "Not a thing did I see on the road, but Mr Smellie driving to Dunbar," said Aunt Jane composedly. (Mr Smellie was parish minister of Innerwick.) "Well", said Mother "How ungentlemanly of him to drive past without offering to take you in." "Take me in!" exclaimed Aunt Jane wrathfully, "Would I be seen driving with an Established Church minister! Smellie knew his place better than to ask me," finished she scornfully. But as the years glided on, Aunt Jane modified her opinions, as did others, and very wisely too. For indeed, the uncharitableness of both sides must have done great harm, and the old saying, "See how these Christians love one another", might oftener have been read "hate."

THE FREE CHURCH OF SCOTLAND

John Freeland was appointed minister of the Free Church, Innerwick in 1845, and there he still is, consequently this year, 1895, is his Jubilee. He was the first minister ordained by the Glasgow Free Church Presbytery. Aunt Jane gladly acted as his housekeeper for many years, paying frequent visits to us, Calder Park, and her numerous friends, for she was, as I have said, extremely popular. To the schemes of the Free Church, my father gave largely. With six other gentlemen, he bound himself to build 20 churches in out-the-way places, and accomplished it too. As I said of our aunts, so I say of him, all the good he did was quietly done. His mind was, however, perfectly free from bigotry, and he was open to see good in all denominations.

I think in many ways, he was like his friend George (afterwards Sir George, Baronet) Burns. He, a son of Dr Burns of the Barony, by little and little, found the service of the Church of England had such power over him that he could no longer remain a Presbyterian. My father did not go so far, but he greatly appreciated the beautiful Liturgy of the Church.

Jane Anne and Maggie had always gone with Mother to St Mary's Episcopal Church[104] in Glasgow, my father continuing to go to St David's,[105] of which Dr Lorimer was minister; but after I was born, he began to think we must be brought up in either one church or the other. He made up his mind, therefore, to go to the Episcopal Church. In the meantime, Mother had been considering the same subject, and she made up her mind to go with him. Being the more impulsive of the two, she spoke first. The only stumbling block to her was Dr Lorimer, whose preaching she did not like. It was settled at last by my dear father saying that if she could find a minister to her liking he would gladly accept her offer of going to the Free Church with him, but in no way would he force her to do so. She very much liked Dr Samuel Miller of St Matthew's so it ended up by them going there. But I am always a little sorry, that in this instance Mother "spoke first."

Now some may think that my dear parents' views of church matters were lax. I do not think so. I think, rather, that they showed the spirit of Christ. And yet I, who have been brought up as an Episcopalian from the age of 14, am thoroughly staunch to my own dear Church, I could never be a Presbyterian, but I do see, and gladly acknowledge, that there is good to be found in every branch of the Christian Church. "We all try to serve the same Master", said a little Roman Catholic nun to me once; and so saying, kissed me gently. And as I looked into her sweet, pure eyes, I felt sure that she did "try", and no doubt succeeded.

I was once as a small child very angry at having old Mr Duncan, the tenant in the farm of Bandeath, say to Grandpapa, "Wright would as soon have put his foot into a pail of scalding water as enter an English Chapel." I told this directly Papa and Mama came in the main grievance to me being the farmer's disrespect in saying Wright, in place of Mr Wright. "Oh", laughed Papa. "he little knows how nearly 'Wright' joined the English Chapel altogether." "What a pity I spoke first", said Mother mischievously (you must remember, dear children, that any Episcopal Church at that time was looked upon, and spoken of, as a chapel in this Presbyterian land).

104 St Mary's was in Renfield Street in the 1840s.

105 St David's, Ramshorn, Ingram Street.

The very first thing that I can remember happened when I was two years and nearly two months old. It may be said that so young a child could not remember, but it is a fact that I do.

Mr Gladstone states that he remembers distinctly when he was only eighteen months old, helping himself upstairs by holding on to his nurse's dress. He even remembers the flowered pattern of the chintz of which the dress was made; and says it was proved that he was only eighteen months old, because the nurse in question left his parents' service when he was just about that age.

My first memory is of a Saturday, October 28th 1848, when we were all at dinner in the nursery. Jenny Welsh came in with a beaming face, and said we were all to go downstairs to see a new baby. Nurse Margaret, in great haste, caught me up, and downstairs we all went to Papa's dressing room, and there by the fire sat Menie, and on her capacious knee, lay a little baby; and this baby, dear Isobel and Leslie, was your own dear Mother. We were not allowed to stay more than a minute or two, and then Nurse Margaret hurried us all off to finish our dinners. So you see, my very first memory is a very happy thing.

MARY'S CHRISTENING/ALL ILL OF WHOOPING COUGH

As soon as Menie left, the new baby was given over to a Highland woman, Margaret Buchanan, from Easdale, to nurse. For I had been such a delicate creature brought up by hand. Nurse Buchanan, as we called her, proved very devoted to her little charge, and it was really owing to her care that our sweet Mary lived; for, soon after she was born, we all took whooping-cough, and when the feeble little thing was nearly strangled with phlegm, the good woman put her mouth to the baby's, and, by suction, drew up the phlegm. She said she had seen this done to a sick lamb in Easdale.

This baby was christened by Uncle Munro and received the name of Mary Eliza, Mary after Mother's much loved sister Mrs Duthie, Eliza after the no less dear Eliza Wright at Calder Park. Jane Ann remembers our all being wrapped in shawls because of our cough, and taken to see Mary christened, but this I do not remember, as I soon became very ill not only from whooping-cough, but from congestion of the lungs, so ill that Dr Rainy[106] quite despaired of saving me, and tried some desperate remedy as a last resource. He gave the dose, whatever it was, and told Mother to walk up and down with me in her arms, and on no account let me sleep. Up and down went poor Mother, and at last a rush of blood came from me, and she nearly dropped me in her fright; but Dr Rainy exclaimed, "She is saved!" and slowly

---

106 Dr Harry Rainy was one of the foremost physicians in Glasgow. He was also Professor of Forensic Medicine in the University 1841-1872. He died in 1876.

I struggled back to life. So too did Mary; but Maggie, who had not been nearly so ill, never gained strength even after the cough left her, but fell into what the old people used to call "a decline", dear, beautiful Maggie.

DEATH OF MRS WRIGHT OF CALDER PARK

A cloud of sorrow hung over the whole family then, for Grandmamma at Calder Park lay dying, not ill of any particular disease, but just "wearing awa." Her death took place Dec. 6th. 1848. Aunt Eliza made notes of some of her last words, and the verses and hymns which she repeated. A copy of them, she gave to my father, and he kept it carefully. Hers had been a very happy life, and she liked to say so. "What am I that Thou carest for me", she said, "surely goodness and mercy have followed me all the days of my life." And she bid her children "pray for your mother, she prayed for you when you were not able to pray for yourselves"; and doubtless as she said this, she would think of the days when she "happed them in their wee beds a', and "blest them round and round."

Aunt Eliza writes, "She exhorted her friends to be in earnest, to seek the one thing needful and kindly admonished her grandchildren who were about her. And also with great composure and firmness gave directions about her funeral etc. One day when very weak (and the last time she was out of her room), she expressed a wish to have her family all around her, and said, "I desire to clasp you all in my arms, and take you all with me! Good is the will of the Lord, God's time is the best time. Not my will but Thine be done!" The good, tender, old mother! One can well understand her "longing to take them all with her."

Once she said, "This will soon be all over, and when I get home, the first I expect to meet will be my Saviour, then your Father, Janet, and all the little ones who have gone before; what a happy meeting that will be; and I hope you will all soon follow." In speaking of her married life, she said, "What a happy home I have had here, few, perhaps, happier, for such a Husband, and such a Parent as you had, you little knew. What am I that I have been so cared-for all of my life!" Then, thinking of the God and Saviour Whom she had so faithfully striven to serve, she said, "Thou art the chiefest among ten thousand, and altogether lovely. Draw out the desires of my soul toward Thee. Lord, thou knowest all things, Thou knowest that I love Thee. Make me Thine now, and Thine for ever. May Thy Rod and Thy Staff be with me whilst passing through the dark valley and the shadow of death, and I will fear no evil; and underneath be the everlasting arms to support and comfort me." At another time, thinking of the dear ones she was leaving, she prayed, "May we all meet around God's Holy Throne not one wanting." On the Sunday evening before her death, she sang in a clear voice:

"Into Thine hands I do commit
My Spirit; for thou art He,
O thou Jehovah, God of Truth,
That hast redeemed me."

And not many days after, so praying, so singing, with holy thoughts in her heart, and holy words on her lips, she "fell on sleep", and, awaking, would see, I doubt not, her Saviour, husband, Janet, and the little ones, so dear to her.

PERSONAL RECOLLECTIONS: MY APOLOGY

And now, my dear Isobel and Leslie, from this date all that I write will be from my own recollections. There will, of necessity be a great deal of myself in the "memories", but that is unavoidable; and also many of the stories I shall tell you may be quite differently told to you by your Mother and Auntie Jean, though substantially the same. But then you must remember that people look upon things from a totally different point of view; the points that one person takes up and dwells upon are often totally overlooked by another. Each one has a different stand-point; each one has a different range of vision, above all, each one has a different individuality; and this same individuality imprints itself very distinctly on every narration of facts or events, written or told. Take for example the four Evangelists, they all wrote the life of Our Lord, but how differently! Some of them tell the same stories, but with apparent discrepancies. Why? Because they looked upon the occurrence from a different point of view. And on every gospel is imprinted the style, mode of thought, or in short the individuality of the writer. Therefore, dear children, though everything I write shall be absolutely true, yet the events I record, the characters I describe, the motives I assign to people, must necessarily be coloured by me, as I saw them, I heard them, I imagined them to be. This is my apology for the I, me, mine, that will so often appear in all I record.

As I told you, the year 1848 was a sad one for our family, first in the death of Grandmamma at Livelands, and then the death of Grandmamma at Calderpark. The bright event was the birth of little Mary; but then came the anxiety of the whooping cough, and then the fading away of sweet Maggie.

But first I must say that at that time, we, in common with all other children of gentle folks, called our father and mother Papa and Mamma. Indeed it was thought old-fashioned, if not plebeian to do otherwise. The children of the working classes never then used those names; and I remember as a little girl at Livelands seeing the look of astonishment upon Christie the gardener's daughter Jeanie, when Papa said to her, "How is your Mamma?." Jeanie stared, and said nothing, and Mother whispered, "She doesn't know what you mean." But the wheel of fashion turns completely round; and now we of the upper classes say only father and mother, and the little gutter children say papa and mamma. But in writing of the days of our childhood I shall use the old familiar names by which we then addressed our parents.

FUNERALS

I told you my first recollection was of Mary's birth. After that I do not remember anything, because we all became ill. Grandmamma died at Calder

Park, and we all had black frocks, even baby Mary wore a grey "carrying cloak", (this cloak of your mother's, we still have, dear Isobel and Leslie), mourning being very much more de rigeur than now. Women literally covered their dresses, cloaks, and bonnets with crepe, and as to men, their hats not only had crepe bands up to the very top, but enormous bows of crepe behind, which made them look top-heavy. They also wore broad, white, fine, muslin hem-stitched cuffs sewn on to the sleeves of their coats, called "weepers." After the first Sunday after a funeral, these were covered with crepe, so that the white showed through. As to the funerals, they were appalling, the horses shrouded in black, the hearses surmounted in huge black nodding plumes, and before the horses walked two or three men, called "Soulies", but for what reason, except to heighten the effect by their streaming hat-bands of black if the dead person were old or middle-aged, white if it were a child or a young person, I know not. People wore deep mourning long after their friends' death. How changed it all is now! Sometimes it seems to me as if people were in too great a hurry to don again bright colours. But one should not judge.

LETTERS TO MAGGIE AT LIVELANDS 1848

Maggie and I were at Livelands with Nurse Margaret in the autumn of 1848 and Jane Anne writes a letter to Maggie, or rather dictates it for it is in Mother's handwriting, and she must have held Jane Anne's hand when she signed it. It is addressed to Miss Margaret W. Wright, Livelands.

"Dear Sissy, I hope you are quite well. I am going to buy you a pretty picture book, and Isabella one too. I was up at the Necropolis, and saw the place where Mr Buchanan was buried.

I am real fond of the Pussy, it is called Tom Tod. I was up in the nursery, and it looked very bare. I was out in the garden, but it is not pretty. I am coming home soon. Write me a letter. Give little Baby a kiss, and Nurse Margaret. Your affectionate sister, Jane Anne."

LETTER TO MAGGIE 1848

Maggie got two letters at Livelands on her birthday. Mother writes,

"Dear Margaret Wilsone, Many happy returns of the 5th of October. I hope you are a good little girl, and now that you are four years old you will give up picking your fingers. I have sent you a Sunday book, and a picture book, some French sweeties, and a pair of gloves. I have also sent a parcel to Jane Anne and Isabella, and I hope you will all be kind to one another, and if you are good Nurse Margaret will read the story books to you. I meant to have sent you a cake for tea, but it is so wet I cannot get out to buy it, but will send down one when Papa goes to see you. Goodbye, my dear pets, and Believe me, your affectionate Mamma, Isabella W. Wright. I will write to Jane Anne next time."

"Calder Park, 5th of October, 1848. Aunt Eliza has been thinking much about dear Margaret Wilsone today, now four years old. What a big girl you must be growing. I have no doubt I would be quite astonished if I saw you. I send you a nice little book about Jesus changing the heart. I hope, my dear child, you will pray to Jesus many times every day to give you "a new heart and a right spirit," that you may love and serve Jesus here. You will then be happy here, and when you die Jesus will take you to that "happy land" that your little hymn tells you about, where you shall sing glory, glory, for ever more. Give Aunt Eliza's best love to Jane Anne and Isabella Murray. She desires the same blessings for them; and is longing greatly to see her dear little girls. Aunt Eliza hopes that Nurse Margaret is quite well, and getting on nicely since Papa and Mamma left. Maggie Munro sends kiss and love to her cousins, and is wearying to see them. Grandmamma, Aunt Margaret, and Aunt Eliza send much love to Jane Anne, Margaret Wilsone, and Isabella Murray. Ever, my dear child, your affectionate Aunt, Eliza Wright."

There is one other little letter to Maggie, printed no doubt painfully and laboriously by Maggie Munro, on December 16th.

"My dear Maggie, I am happy to hear that you are able to be downstairs, with your neck bare. Give my love to Miss Sawers, I am your cousin Margaret W. Munro."

MAGGIE 1848

Miss Sawers was Jane Anne's governess. She left us to be married to Mr Stark. The "bare neck" to which Maggie Munro alludes, was the low-bodied frock always worn by children in those days; summer and winter, the little necks and arms were bare. It was very pretty to see the soft, pretty little arms and necks, but how many children must have died of the exposure! Our Maggie was a merry little thing. She generally went by the name of "the Quaker's Wife", because she used to dance, and sing,

> *"Merrily danced the Quaker's Wife,*
> *Merrily danced the Quaker"*

an old song, the rest of which I have forgotten.

Once when we were at Calder Park, we were taken to see a poor, bedridden man, James Walker, who lived in a little cottage on the Tandlemuir, a lonely place, standing high, with a fine view. James had a spine complaint, and could not move, but he was carefully tended by his old sister May, and his niece Mysie, and the cottage was exquisitely clean. Maggie's little tender heart was touched by the sight of the invalid, and when she was going away, she trotted up to the bedside, and held up her face to be kissed. Greatly surprised and gratified was James, and years after, he told us about the kiss "the little lady" had given him. When I was about 11 years old, I was sitting by him, eating a huge slice of bread and butter cut for me by May, and gazing the while out of the cottage windows at the lovely view. "You are admiring the view", he said, "When I look at it, I always say to myself, "Ah Lord God, behold Thou hast made the heavens and the earth by Thy great power and stretched-out arm, and there's nothing too hard for Thee", and he handed me his Bible and told me, in the good old Scots fashion, to read it for myself in Jer. 32. 17. And as I did so, I heard him whisper again, "Nothing too hard for Thee." And I have often in my heart thanked good James Walker for teaching me that verse. I have remembered it when I looked at beautiful scenery, and comforted myself with it in times of perplexity.

Maggie's delicacy increased day by day, and at last she was too weak to leave her little bed. Mother told me that I sat on the bed beside her, and we played together, but the time came when she could not play. It was thought not good for a little young child like me to be always with one so ill, so they tried again and again to keep us apart. But it was no use, Maggie would cry and say, "Where's Lillabella, (her name for me) I can't do without Lillabella." And I, brought back, would run to her with little outstretched hands and say, "Here me, my wee pettie!" This is the name I called her.

MAGGIE'S DEATH 1848

There was nothing wonderful about Maggie, no precocious saying such as we used to read in the marvellous lives of children who died young (and who must, I think, have been horrible little prigs!) Maggie was just a merry, natural child, with the loving heart; but Mother had taught her carefully, and stored her little mind with Bible stories. "Take this child and train it for me", is no doubt said by God to every mother, and faithfully ours performed her task. Night after night, she sat by the child, and read to her from "The Peep of Day." "Sometimes", she told me, I had hardly any voice to read, but Maggie would beg, "O read to me about Jesus, Mamma." She could never hear the story of our Lord's Crucifixion without crying, dear little one. "O not that, not that, it makes me cry", she said. She talked about the garden at Calder Park, and asked Mother to tell Aunt Margaret to come and see her, and to bring her "some green peas." It was early for peas, but Aunt Margaret gathered some very young ones, and hurried off to see her darling. But by the time she arrived, Maggie was too ill to eat peas, though she liked to know Aunt Margaret had brought them.

Mother said as the end drew near, another attempt was made to take me away, but it distressed Maggie so much, that it was given up. She said Maggie used to pray for me, "O God", the little voice prayed, "Bless Lillabella, and make her a good girl." And she was so in earnest as she said it, that sometimes she cried. And on the 15th of June, God took her to Himself. Of course I could not understand that she died, if I thought about it at all I would think she was asleep. But she went away with my kisses on her sweet face; and when she arrived at home, and the Good Shepherd took His little lamb in His Arms to bless her, perhaps she would lay her curly head on His bosom, and tell Him about Lillabella, poor Lillabella, so very lonely without her "wee pettie."

There are some little ones, so gentle, so tender, that they could never travel long over the rough places of life. Their sweet eyes would fill with tears, their pretty lips would quiver at the first harsh word. I think our Maggie was one of those. And the Loving Father knew this, so He only gave her a very little journey, and the sun shone all the way, and she knew nothing but love. For look you, my dears, God leads us by very different ways to Himself. Some are so feeble that they cannot climb very quickly, they have to be led by quiet paths, and encouraged at every step. They are afraid of everything, and are apt wail and be piteous. With such, God is very patient, "He knoweth our frame." Others are so strong that they scorn the winding, up-hill road, and try to scale the rocks. And sometimes they are allowed to do this. But they grow giddy, and fall. If, when they fall, they cry to God, they are helped, and go on again. But alas! there are some that are too proud to cry. These turn, and go down the hill. And there are some that when they fall never attempt to rise. Over them, the angels weep.

Then there are others who sing as they go; and these, strange to say, are often among the heavy-laden, yet - they sing! It is not a very loud song, how could it be, the way being so steep, and the burden so heavy, it is generally,

> *"a tender, cradling measure, soft and low,*
> *not sad, nor long, but such as we remember long ago."*

There is a little pause sometimes, and then there is a "De Profundis", but soon the sweet, clear song breaks out again. And it is wonderful how fellow-travellers are cheered by this singing. The sorrowful smile a little, though but for a moment. The bad man listens, and it may be, thinks of his mother. And one who has fallen by the way, gets up, and prays, and totters on again. And these sweet singers sometimes sing even as they enter the dark valley. We hear it far off, and wonder, and say, "it is the very lovely song of one that hath a pleasant voice." And then the song ceases - for us. But is continued before the Throne of God. Our Maggie sang, all through her little journey, and the memory of her song lingered in the hearts of those that loved her.

Maggie's little wasted body was laid in the coffin, and carried down to the parlour beside the drawing room, and there every morning after prayers, Nurse Margaret used to go in to look at her, and weep, taking me with her. I was not the least afraid, I did not understand what it was to be dead, Maggie was lying there, asleep. It was worse when Nurse Margaret picked me up, and carried me to the nursery where she was not. I took possession of her little chair, and sat still and quiet. It was a pretty little basket chair, comfortably padded covered all over with red. I remember the funeral day. Mother, the aunts, Jane Ann, Maggie Munro, Nurse Margaret and myself were all in the drawing room. Mother sat in one window, in an agony of grief, and Aunt Agnes stood by her, patting her all the while, and saying "dear Isabella, poor thing." I was in Nurse Margaret's arms close to Mother, and when the little coffin was carried out, Mother put back the blind, to see the last of her darling; and I saw Papa get into the mourning coach with Uncle John, and the coffin was laid upon his knees, and he put his arms over it.

Maggie was buried in the old burying ground of Glasgow Cathedral. Aunt Janet lies there too, and so does Papa. Some years ago, it was closed for interments according to the new sanitary laws about church yards in towns.

MAGGIE'S POSSESSIONS - THE DIAMOND RING

I have three little letters of Maggie's, her tiny silver thimble, a little oval, white and red doll's plate, and a small book with her name on it. The little basinette she slept in as a baby, with green silk curtains, was given away when we left St Vincent Street, so too was the cot (crib it was called in our day) in which she died. I have the ring with her hair in it, which Mother wore, also the diamond ring with her name, age 4 years, 8 months, and date of her death engraved on the inside. It was the custom then to wear a ring in memory of a dead friend or relative. Five or ten pounds were often bequeathed "to buy a mourning ring." They were generally black and heavy. Grandpapa had a beautiful diamond breast pin given to him by Mrs McLeod of Raasay. When Maggie died he gave it to Mother to be made in to a ring to wear in memory of Maggie. It is set in gold with black enamel. Mother wore it next to her wedding ring, and shortly before her death, she took it from her finger (a thing I had never seen her do before, for she wore it night and day) and said, "Put it on, dear, I want to see how it looks on your finger. When I am away, I want you to wear Maggie's ring, there are only you and I left that loved her." Something in the way Mother said this made me burst into tears. I put on the ring, and she added, "if I go first, you must wear this ring in memory of me; and if you go first I shall wear this one," touching the topaz and pearl one which had been an ear-ring of her mother's "in memory of you." So you can understand, dear children, how much I value this diamond ring.

A pair of Maggie's little shoes, her name marked on the soles, Mother kept among her treasures. I have a doll of hers, a small rag one, made by Mother, dressed like a fashionable gentleman of the time in black velvet coat, red waistcoat, and white trousers. His name was Timothy Pickleback. Aunt Jane taught me these lines that she said she always associated with Maggie.

"That lovely child, so fresh and fair, called hence by an early doom,
Just came to show how sweet a flower, in Paradise could bloom."

I suppose after Maggies death, I was washed and dressed and put to bed as usual, but I can recall nothing, but sitting still in her chair, and feeling alone.

Parents and aunts were all in great grief, as to Nurse Margaret she was overwhelmed. So probably she was only too glad that I sat still and did not trouble her; besides I had always been a quiet little creature. Children were expected then "to be seen and not heard", and the Reign of Children, which now in the end of the century, is a veritable Reign of Terror to old fashioned people, had not even dawned, certainly it never did in our nursery.

DR RAINY - MARY TO BE MY BABY

Mother and Aunt Eliza told me that they got a great shock one day. Doctor Rainy had come to see Mary who was teething, and he stood before my little chair, and surveyed my listless attitude; then turned sharply, and said to them, "You have lost one child already, see that you don't lose another. That child is dying of grief." Dear Mother said when she told me this, "You don't know what I suffered, to think that I had neglected you!"

But is was not that, it was only that they had not realised I was so sorrowful. She asked Dr Rainy what she should do. "Rouse her, try to get her to take to the baby." He was an abrupt old man, though his heart was kind. (His beautiful likeness, an engraving, hangs in our dining room.) So Mary was brought to me, and I was told she was to be my baby, that I must love her, and play with her, and (according to the custom of the time; which always "pointed a moral" even to the very callow young) set her a good example by being a good little girl myself. And bit by bit my love for the sweet little thing grew and grew, till it filled my little heart. Mother said when she saw how passionately I attached myself to her, she trembled less anything should befall Mary, and then what would have become of me! Poor Mother had been told by an old minister, Doctor Nathaniel Paterson, "Keep a loose grip on the children, Mrs Wright, they are but frail little things after all"; she reminded me of this when you were a baby, sweet Isobel, and added kindly, "Don't set your heart too much on her, dear."

Papa felt Maggie's death terribly. He had very keen feelings, and she had wound herself round his heart. Cousin John Freeland remembers walking up the street behind St Vincent Street, from which the nursery windows are seen, with Papa, two years after she died. He noticed he became silent, and asked, "Is there anything wrong"? "John", he said, "I can never walk up this street without thinking I should see that darling little child at the window." Maggie used to wave to him from the nursery window.

AT CALDER PARK 1850

Papa and Mamma with Jane Anne, went to England in 1850, to the marriage of Jane Duthie and the Rev. Martin Edgar Benson (married, July 16th). Jane Anne, then 8 years old, was one of the bridesmaids. They were away two or three months, and Mary and I spent the time first at Calder Park then at Livelands, Nurse Margaret of course being with us. By that time there was no under nurse, as Nurse M. decided she would rather do the work herself a hundred times, than for ever fechting with these! It was early in the summer that we went to Calder Park, for the sweet white lilies, "sweet Nancies", is their old fashioned name, were in flower. I was very happy there. The four aunts, for Aunt Jane was at home on a visit, did their best to make me happy, they had so grieved over my sorrows in losing Maggie.

But there I must stop in my story to say how wisely dear Mother and everyone else about me behaved in what they told me about her. They never in any way deceived me with false comforts; they let me know clearly that she was dead, and that I should never see her in this world again, but if I were good, I should meet her in heaven. I feel so strongly that little children should never be deceived, especially by their mothers. For, if a child once distrusts its mother, then, Heaven help it! For it is but a very little step to distrust its God.

Perhaps I should not have remembered this time so clearly, but for the joys of that dear old garden. Mary was able to toddle about with me, and we spent hours there. Aunt Mary, in a shady bonnet, was generally at work in her flower beds, and there were certain beds where we were allowed to gather the flowers. I revelled in the big bed of white lilies, some of the aunts objected to the strong scent in the house, so I might gather as many as I pleased. The aunts kept me a good deal with them, and occasionally Nurse Margaret swooped down and declared I was being spoilt. And it was then that when I was in disgrace in the nursery, I used to fly to Aunt Jane, and bury my face in her lap. She always called me "her child" in consequences of this, and after her death Aunt Eliza told me I had always been her favourite niece.

The hens, the cows, the pig and Newfoundland dog Bevis (he was succeeded by Flash) chained to his kennel in the yard, were all delightful to country-loving me. Agnes Aitken was the house maid, and Izbel Laird, commonly called Bell, the cook. Izbel went to Calder Park the same year 1842, that Jenny came to us, and she stayed there till the last of the "ladies" died in 1882. She died herself not long after. Twice a week, Izbel churned. Churns were then tall wooden things, with an instrument (I think it was called a splasher) that was worked up and down. It must have been hard work, churning in those days.

The only grievance I had at this time, was that the days flew so fast. One day I was watching Aunt Margaret wind up the big eight day clock. "What is the thing that wags?", I asked, "why does it wag?", "If it didn't wag, the clock would stop, and then we couldn't tell the time," said she, and obligingly caught "the thing that wagged", to show me how the whole clock stopped, "If it didn't wag Nurse Margaret wouldn't know when to put you to bed my dear." Dear, innocent, unsuspecting Aunt Margaret! In my little heart I at once determined to prevent the catastrophe of going to bed, and lengthen the happy days by stopping the clock. So at the first opportunity, when no one was about, I opened the little door of the clock; and boldly caught "the thing that wagged." The silence was a little alarming, but I scrambled up the steep stair to the nursery quite satisfied. A great commotion soon got up, what was wrong with the clock, it had never stopped before, Aunt Margaret and Izbel were quite piteous. I listened in horror, then burst into tears. "What ails ye"? said Nurse Margaret, with a little shake to my shoulder, (she often emphasised her words with little shakes and pats), and I sobbed out, "I did it, I stopped it, the days are so short." I think she was very much amused, for she picked me up in her arms without scolding me, and carried me down to the aunts. "Now tell why you did it", she said. "The days are so short, and I am so happy here", I wailed. And oh, the kissing and hugging that followed. "To think that the dear child is so happy, she wanted to lengthen the days." And never, even when I was grown up, did Aunt Margaret forget to remind me of how pleased they were when I stopped "the thing that wagged", because the days were too short at Calder Park.

LIVELANDS 1850

After some time, we two little ones and Nurse Margaret went to Livelands, where we stayed till Papa and Mamma and Jane Anne returned from England. I fell down the drawing room stair from top to bottom one day, and landed on the top of old Rover, so was not much hurt, but when Nurse Margaret lifted me up, she thought my foot had got in between the stair railing, and so was sprained by her suddenly pulling me up. Very likely I had fallen with it doubled under me, but I screamed with pain, and could not stand, and she, poor dear woman, was in agony thinking she had hurt me. Grandpapa sent for old Doctor Johnston, but he did not think there was much wrong; still I could not even stand. So Grandpapa had me taken to Danny Ferguson, the famous "bone doctor."[107] He ordered a poultice of some of his herbs, and Menie Mackenzie and Nurse Margaret put it on too hot, and my poor little foot was badly burnt, and still bears the mark of it. They thought I was only crying because I did not like the poultice, and I remember how kind they both were, and how Menie told me her famous story about a certain Tibbie who had a pen knife, a grand possession. I am quite sure Menie and Nurse Margaret suffered much more than I did, when they found I had had such good cause to cry.

KILMUN 1850

When Papa and Mamma and Jane Anne came home, we all went to Oakbank, Strone Point, Kilmun, on the Holy Loch. Kilmun derives its name from the Abbot Mundas, or Munna. He lived between 700 and 730. The Holy Loch is so called, because there a ship was wrecked, returning with earth

---

107 Daniel Ferguson (1803-1888) was a native of Stirling, educated at Glasgow, and held in high esteem for his skill throughout Stirlingshire. The Smith has a marble portrait bust, and there is a fine bronze portrait bas-relief plaque on his tomb in the Valley Cemetery, Stirling.

from the Holy Land, which was to have been scattered over the spot where on to build Glasgow Cathedral. Aunt Eliza and Maggie Munro came to stay with us.

There dear Mother taught me a little lesson that I never forgot. Maggie and Jane Anne told her I was afraid in the dark. "O but there is nothing to be afraid of, come and I will show you." So we went into the drawing room where the shutters were closed, and she shut the door. "Now there's nothing to be afraid of, God is with you in the dark", and holding my little hand, (how I clung to her!) she led me round and round the table, till somehow, because I trusted her, all the fear vanished. I think now I hear the comforting tone of her voice, and her assurance that God was there as in the light, sank deep into my mind. I have thought since then of Faber's lines in connection with the little scene;

> *"Thy greatness makes us bold as children are,*
> *When those they love are nigh."*

In these days when the means of locomotion are so varied and easy, it is curious to recall the days when rail roads were only in their infancy. Mails used to be carried on horseback, or in mail carts at an average speed of 3´ miles an hour. On July 7. 1788, the first London Mail pulled up at the Saracen's Head Glasgow, surrounded by a crowd of horsemen who had ridden out to meet it. The Caledonian Railway was opened between Glasgow and London in Feb. 15. 1848. When Stevenson was asked what would happen if a cow got in front of a train, he answered dryly, "It would be bad for the coo!"

THE GREAT EXHIBITION OF 1851

In 1851, gold was discovered in Australia which before that year had not been much more than a penal settlement to receive our convicts. Botany Bay was the place to which they were generally sent, There was a great rush from this country to the gold diggings, and many fortunes were made. The first great International Exhibition was opened in London in May, 1851. It was entirely owing to Prince Albert that such a great and wise undertaking was ever planned. Of its glories and success, I need not write. A full description with pictures will be found in the bound volume of the Illustrated London News. Our father and mother went to see it, leaving us children at Oak Bank, Strone Point, with Nurse Margaret and some of the Calder Park aunts.

DAGUERROTYPES

It was while in London at that time, that our father and mother had their likenesses taken by the new process invented by Monsieur Louis Daguerre, and called a "daguerreotype" in honour of the inventor.[108] We still have these two likenesses and very comical they are compared with the beautiful

114

photographs we now have. The process of being "taken" was a most trying one. The unfortunate person had to stare at a pin stuck in a white sheet on which the sun shone fiercely. Could "a pleased expression", or, at least, a natural one, be the result under such trying circumstances? How odd to our eyes now the dress of that period appears! Mother wears a bonnet of large dimensions, and inside it, round her face, a perfect garden of roses.

We children had our daguerreotypes taken in Glasgow when Jane Anne was about ten; I, six; and Mary four years old. They were taken by Jabez Hughes, who afterwards went to Ryde in the Isle of Wight and became the Queen's photographer. Mary's likeness, as you, dear Isabel and Lesley have often said, is quite charming. She wears a little green frock with brown spots on it made with a low neck and short sleeves. She has short socks, and black shoes. Her lips are parted in a smile, which shows her lovely little teeth, so even and white that Aunt Eliza used to call her "Miss White-Teeth." She was terribly shy, poor little dear, and looked so grave that Jabez Hughes feared he would not be able to get a nice likeness of her, till Mother picked up a tambourine and played on it, and danced; and this amazing sight (for in those days mothers did not caper before their offspring), made Mary smile broadly. I can quite recall her telling me herself in the nursery about this and saying, "Mamma danced, Mamma, just think!"

NURSERY DAYS

Everyone when middle life is reached is apt to look back to youthful days, and to say "how different things were when I was a child"! No doubt this remark has been made in every age, but things had certainly changed very completely in the last 50 years, and especially as regards the training of children. The endurance, obedience, and respect for our elders and betters instilled into children in former days, must have had a good effect in forming their characters, and fitting them for the tear and wear of after years. A modern child put into our old nursery under Nurse Margaret's strict rule, would probably object very much. To us, it was quite natural and proper, and we were perfectly happy. Looking back upon it, however, I can see that we were certainly "contented wi' little", compared to what a child now would require to make it happy.

Mary and I were by no means model children, but we were gentle, law abiding creatures, and having been trained from our earliest infancy to obey, it never once occurred to us to dispute Nurse Margaret's authority, and she was an excellent nurse. It was her pride and pleasure to hear people ask who made our dainty little garments and to remark upon our spotless cleanliness. Oh how we were scrubbed! What washing, and combing and brushing of hair, what changing of frocks and even little unmentionables every day before she sent us down to the dining room for

---

108 Louis Daguerre (1789-1851) took the first 'daguerrotype' photograph in 1839.

"dessert" as was then the custom for little children after their parents had dined. Arrived at the door, it was opened wide for us by Margaret Morrison the table maid (now Mrs Macarthur) and hand in hand we trotted in, stopping just inside the door to make a deep curtsey, with the left foot well behind, and holding out our little frocks with each hand. How funny and prim it sounds now and yet it must have been pretty. We then had a biscuit, and a fig, or grapes. Generally a game of "spillicans",[109] and then Nurse Margaret rang the nursery bell, and we went back to the nursery where we each had a small "coggie"[110] of porridge and milk and then got ready for bed.

Mother used to come to the nursery then, and she heard us say our prayers. Very simple they were, "O God, bless Papa and Mamma, my two little sisters, and all kind friends, and make me a good girl for Jesus Christ's sake, Amen." Then "Suffer the little children to come unto me" etc. And the old lines,

> *"This night I lay me down to sleep,*
> *I pray the Lord my soul to keep,*
> *If I should die before I wake,*
> *I pray the Lord my soul to take", Amen.*

Dear old lines, learnt in baby days! I say them still every night. I was interested to read in the life of Archibald Tait, Archbishop of Canterbury, that he, too, said them nightly all his days; and one of his brothers, a soldier, did the same; and on more than one occasion, sleeping on the bare ground, under foreign skies, the old words came to his lips, taught to him long ago by his mother at Harvistoun Castle, (Dollar). It is the things that we learn in early youth, that we never forget.

THE OLD SCOTS SONGS

Nurse Margaret kept the nursery cheery by her singing. She had a pretty voice, and knew all the good old Scots songs. And how beautiful they are, how full of wit, of love, of tenderness, of pathos. Mary and I used to sit in our little chairs each side of the nursery fire, and listen to her with delight. We laughed over "The Laird of Cockpen", "Johnny Cope" and such like, and cried over "The Flowers of the Forest", and "Lizzie's Flittin." "Dinna greet, bonny lass that I am gaun to leave ye, I'll tak a stick into my hand, and come again and see ye", was what she used merrily to sing to comfort me when I was suffering agonies of fear that someone might fall in love with her, and want to marry her. A favourite song was the wailing Highland lament, "Farewell to Fuinary."

---

109 Spillicans was a game played with small sticks. The Smith has a spillicans set in its collection.

110 A wooden bowl.

"The wind is fair, the day is fine,
Swiftly, swiftly runs the time;
The boat is floating on the tide
That wafts me off from Fuinary.

Eirich agus tuigainn O,
Eirich agus tuigainn O,
Eirich agus tuigainn O,
Mo shoraidh slan le Fionn Airidh

A thousand, thousand tender ties
Accept this day my plaintive sighs;
My heart within me almost dies
At thoughts of leaving Fiunary

Eirich agus tuigainn O,
Eirich agus tuigainn O,
Eirich agus tuigainn O,
Mo shoraidh slan le Fionn Airidh"

OLD SONGS AND RHYMES

A particularly cheerful song, and much liked by us, was,

"Auntie Jenny's currant bun,
Auntie Jenny's currant bun,
Gie's a knife to cut a slice,
O' Auntie Jenny's current bun."

Then there were little old fashioned rhymes such as,

"Katie Bairdie had a coo,
Black and white aboot the mou',
Wasna' she a denty coo,
Dance, Katie Bairdie."

And Jenny used to say to us,

"John Smith, fella fine,
Can ye shoe this horse o' mine?
Yes, Sir, that I can,
As weel as ony ither man.
Put a bit upon the tae,
To gar the powney climb the brae,
Put a bit upon the heel,
To gar the powney pace weel, pace weel."

And as she said this, she held my little foot in her hand, patted toe and heel and pretending to "shoe the powney." Another was,

> "Who's that knocking? A Granny dear (grenadier!)
> What do you want? A pint of beer.
> Where's your money? I forgot.
> Get down the stair, you drunken sot."

Mother used to say to us when we put on a new frock for the first time, "What a beau my Granny was, when she went to the fair," part of the words of a very old song.

One of the most determined snuff takers was Queen Charlotte. On one occasion she gave a dance to her young grand-daughter Princess Charlotte and her companions. The Princess was asked to call for a dance. "Tell the band" she said, "to play up 'What a beau my granny was'!" Now the words of that delectable ditty are, or were, for I fear it is now quite forgotten:

> "What a beau my granny was!
> What a beau was she!
> She took snuff, and that's enough!
> And that's enough for me."

> "Oh Father, oh Father I have come to confess, Well, child, well.
> Last night I caught a dish of fish. Well, child, well.
> The cat she stole it out of the dish. Well, child, well.
> I killed the cat. Do penance for that. What penance? Kiss me three times.
> I won't. You shall. I won't. You shall."

This was played by tying two knots on a pocket-handkerchief, slipping the two forefingers into the knots, the one to represent the Father the other the penitent. "Turn about, and wheel about, and jump Jim Crow", Mother and Nurse Margaret used to say when we were being dressed, but who Jim Crow was, is lost in obscurity.

Nurse Margaret did not altogether confine herself to Scots songs, she even attained to classical music, and sang "My Mother bids me bind my hair", (words by Mrs Hunter of Leicester Square) exceedingly well. This she had picked up by listening to Mrs Macnaughton's niece, Mary Smith, singing it in the drawing room. She had another song which she called "Poor Laserree." She did not know the words of it, she used to say. How could she, the words being French! I was greatly amused to discover that "Poor Laserree" was "Partout pour la Syrie", the official melody of the French Empire, composed by Queen Hortense, mother of Napoleon III. Strangely enough, Louis Philippe also adopted it. When we were inclined to be rough with our toys we were reminded,

> "What the children of Holland take pleasure in making,
> The children of England take pleasure in breaking."

And undue appreciation of a new frock, called forth, "the art of dress did ne'er begin, till Eve our mother learnt to sin." You see in those days how much attention was paid to children's morals. When the street lamps were being lit, we said, "Learie, learie light the lamps, long legs and crooked shanks."

There was plenty of music in our young days, both Wrights and Murrays being devoted to it. Aunt Mary used to sing to us if we were tearful, "Said a smile to a tear, on the face of my dear" (by Moore, I think).

Aunt Jane's famous song, greatly appreciated by us, was by Helen Lady Dufferin, written about a real person.

> *"Miss Myrtle is going to be married,*
> *What a number of hearts she will break,*
> *Lord John, Sir Tom, and Sir Harry,*
> *Are a dying of love for her sake."*

And Aunt Eliza had a very sentimental song of olden days,

> *'Gaily the Troubadour touched his guitar,*
> *As he was hastening home from the war'.*

Oh dear, dear singers, all now away! The tears come into my eyes when I recall your old-world songs, and dear voices! Uncle John, Papa's brother, had an exquisite tenor voice. It was a treat to hear him sing. I remember being in the drawing room one evening, and all the guests who had been at dinner besought him to sing, 'My Wife has ta'en the gee' Never, I am sure did his sweet little wife "tak the gee."[111] This is the pretty little song:-

> *"A friend o' mine came here yestereen,*
> *And he wad hae me doun,*
> *To tak' a pint o'ale wi' him,*
> *In the nearest neighbour toun,*
> *But oh indeed, it was, sir,*
> *Sae far the waur for me*
> *For, lang or e'er that I cam' hame*
> *My wife had ta'en the gee.*
>
> *We sat sae late and drank sae stout,*
> *The truth I tell to you,*
> *That, lang or e'er the midnicht came*
> *We a' were roarin' fou'.*
> *My wife sits at the fireside*
> *And the tear blinds aye her e'e*
> *The ne'er a bed wad she gang to*
> *But sit and tak' the gee.*

111 Sulk

In the mornin' sun when I cam' doun,
The ne'er a word she spoke,
But mony a sad and sour look
And aye her heid she'd shake.
'My dear,' quoth I, 'what aileth thee
To look sae sour on me?
I'll never do the like again
If you'll ne'er tak' the gee.

When that she heard, she ran, she flung
Her arms about my neck,
And 20 kisses in a crack,
And, poor wee thing, she grat.
'If you'll ne'er do the like again
But bide at hame wi' me,
I'll lay my life, I'll be the wife
That ne'er tak's the gee.'"

THE OLD SCOTS TONGUE

The old Scots language is dying out. I suppose we should not now like to hear our parlourmaids talk as they used to do when we were children. Still it is a pity. The School Boards are turning out everybody on the same pattern, and soon there will be no individuality, certainly no originality. Nurse Margaret used to say she was going to "mash the tea", meaning to infuse it. An apron was called by servants, a "brat"; a pinafore, a "daidlie." When Nurse Margaret wanted us to go into the other nursery, she told us to "go ben the hoose"; and going out of doors, she called "outbye." A pin cushion was a "preen-cod." I remember shocking Mamma by saying "gie's a preen", as I had heard Jessie Christie, daughter of the gardener at Livelands, say. And once when Mary had on a clean, stiffly starched, white sun bonnet, far back in which her sweet little face looked like a daisy for bonny freshness, Kirsty, the table maid at Livelands failing in being able to kiss her, so stiff was the bonnet, was amused to hear the little thing say regretfully, "far ben, my dear."

Grandpapa always called us "the wee dawties." "Dawtie" is the Scottish equivalent for "darling", but infinitely tender to Scottish ears. And almost the last thing he said to Mother as he lay dying in 1861, was, "the wee dawties will soon be home from school." A clock was generally called a "knock", and the servants would say, "Has it chappit ane yet?" The clocks that hung on the walls, were called "wag-at-the-wa's", an appropriate name. Nurse Margaret's usual affirmative was "acky", and she would say when surprised "Heah, sirs"! A corruption of "faith." "My fegs!", another exclamation had the same origin. The round, wooden stick for stirring the porridge, was called a "spurtle", and when the porridge was dished, happy was she who got the spurtle to lick! The corn was cut with a sickle or hook, pronounced heuk. When Nurse Margaret sent us a message, she told us, "haste ye back again", a common exclamation on hearing a surprising bit of news, was, "the lift will fall and smore the laverock", (ie the sky will fall and smother the lark). But I may hear remark that no English translation can adequately express what we say in Scots. An Englishman once tried to translate the names of some Scottish songs; rendered into English, "Jenny dang the weaver", was "Janet overcame the manufacturer." How common place, how vulgar! It has been truly said that "everything loses by translation except a bishop."

SUPERSTITIONS

Then there were little superstitions, such as putting the poker across the bar of the grate, and so making a cross, this was supposed to make a fire burn well. We were told to shake our pinafores to the new moon, and then we should be rich; never to cut our nails on Sunday or they would not grow again; and dreams troubled dear Nurse Margaret sadly, but she seldom disclosed her visions of the night to us. No doubt they were too "awesome" for young bairns to hear. St Valentine's Day caused a flutter of excitement, not always pleasurable, however. I remember Nurse Margaret weeping and wailing over one sent to her, and the nursery was anything but cheerful that day.

Hallowe'en was duly observed, especially at Livelands, where I remember a large assemblage sitting round the kitchen fire watching the nuts burn; then the blindfolding for clear water, and dirty, and the empty saucer etc. To some of the party, it was a grave and solemn affair, by no means lightly undertaken. Aunt Margaret firmly believed that if a tumbler were broken, the party then in the house, would never all meet again. I was so unfortunate to break one at Calder Park in the autumn of 1859. "Tut, tut, Margaret," said Papa cheerily "don't look so sad." But her fears were realised, for we never did all meet there again, as Papa died in Jan. 1860.

GOVERNESSES

Jane Anne's governess, Miss Sawers, married Mr Stark, and she was succeeded by Miss Telford. As she belonged to Stirling, and all our four maids as well, we children never acquired the horrible Glasgow accent, than which none is more objectionable to my ears. Miss Telford was good and excellent, and did well by Jane Anne, but she was not suited to tiny children like Mary and me. It was at a very early age that our lessons began, indeed I always recall learning; and I know that poor Mary found her yoke so galling that when she was only 4 years old, she determined to rid herself of it by one bold stroke. She made her little curtsey at the door, sweet little one, and then flying into Papa's arms with sobs and wails, announced, "Minna's education is done, Minna's education is done"! in the most determined manner. By which she desired to intimate that she would have no more of it. Now Miss Telford was by no means unkind, but she certainly did not understand little children. Of course Nurse Margaret took our view of the case entirely, and bestowed sympathy on her ain bairns.

I used to fly up the nursery stair and bury my face in her comfortable lap, and speedily forget all the pricks and goads necessary to urge me up the steep ladder to learning, when I heard her kind voice, saying "my wee lammie", "my bonnie wee doo, whisht, whisht, dinna greet." To her credit be it said, she never interfered between us and the governess, nor did we carry any tales. We only wept and were comforted.

When we were still very young a U.P. minister, the Rev. John Maclaren, obligingly fell in love with our governess, and married her. She was succeeded by her younger sister, Miss Cecilia Telford. And I can only say that even now I recall her gentle reign with pleasure; and I delight to kiss her sweet old face, as sweet and as pretty as in those, now, far-away days.

EDUCATION

The methods of teaching were very different then to what they are now; children then learnt everything by heart, a custom which may have had its disadvantages, but it undoubtedly strengthened the memory. The Bible was thoroughly taught; we learnt texts, chapters, psalms, and the Scottish "paraphrases." The 119th psalm, I could repeat from beginning to end, besides many pieces of poetry. I do not think hymns were as popular then as now, and those that were, savoured strongly of "the tomb", which fittingly rhymed with "gloom."

SUNDAY EVENINGS

I remember, young as I was, being struck with the oddity of Mary, aged about 4 or 5, standing with her little hands behind her back saying, "The hour of my departure's come, I hear the voice that calls me home," etc. "But it isn't the hour of her departure", said I, "she is only just come!" And I went off into cackles of mirth, but was gravely called to order for my ill-timed hilarity. This was one Sunday evening when we were, as usual, saying our catechism, psalms and texts to Papa and Mamma. We then read a chapter in the Bible "verse about", and afterwards everyone was expected to repeat a text beginning with A, another with B, and so on through the alphabet, triumphantly finished off by Z, "Zaccheus come down!" Then Mama read aloud part of the "Pilgrim's Progress." How much of the spiritual part entered into our minds I don't know; but assuredly we enjoyed the story. I quaked about the lions, and Giant Despair; admired Greatheart; was awe struck over Apollyon; and tenderly appreciative of Matthew's unholy love of apples. Even now when I take up the dear old book, the same happy feeling comes over me as on those pleasant Sunday evenings.

MUTCHES AND WRAPPERS

For Sunday, though strictly observed, was by no means an uncomfortable day for us little people; indeed once every three weeks it was an especially happy day, that being Jenny's "day in"; and she, to keep us happy and out of mischief while she was busy with lunch, used to take us with her to the kitchen, where we feasted on roasted potatoes with unlimited butter. Perched on high kitchen chairs, eating away, with pewter tea-spoons in our little paws, we enjoyed ourselves excessively, Jenny meantime flitting about in her dainty lilac "wrapper", (servants did not speak of print "dresses" then) and her thick white mutch, as stiff in the full border as it could be, tied under her chin. I think it is a pity that the lilac prints always worn by servants, and the quaint mutches have entirely disappeared. Even Nurse Margaret, though as a nurse she did not wear a cap when "dressed", yet donned a wrapper and mutch for her morning work. It would have been thought impossible for a servant to keep her hair free of dust while sweeping a room, if she had not had her head well enveloped in her mutch. To the end of her days, Jenny wore one. But by degrees, the younger maids left off tying their mutches under their chins, and let their strings hang loose, with a more jaunty air; then the mutch was modified, and did not cover the ears, and the strings were absent; finally the mutch disappeared altogether, and was succeeded by foolish little flat bits of lace, stuck on the very top of the head.

MINISTER'S VISITS TO SERVANTS

The Presbyterian ministers used to have an excellent custom of visiting each one of their congregation at least once in the year. They may still do so, but it does not appear to me that it is as generally done. Formerly it was done with great regularity. Each minister announced from the pulpit the day on which he intended to visit in a certain street or district, and the people were expected to be at home to receive him. All our servants went to different churches, and were duly visited each by her own minister, who was taken by her into the dining room for a short interview alone, after which all the other maids and the children were summoned, a chapter was read and "expounded", followed by a prayer. We used greatly to wish we might be present at the private interview, from a desire to hear if the minister asked the servant to say her catechism, and how she acquitted herself. Children were never brought forward then, and beyond a grave shake of the hand, and a solemn how do you do, not one of the ministers ever bestowed the smallest attention upon us. And yet Mary was a little witch for dainty prettiness, with skin as soft as a peach, and bright eyes, and fair curls. O unappreciative divines!

Some of the Bible readings, either at family prayers, or at some other time, did make an impression on her baby mind; for once in the nursery, she emphatically announced, "Peter Nonay went up to the moon for gathering sticks on the Sabba' Day." "You mustn't say what isn't true", said Jane Ann, but the little one only repeated more strongly her story of the sad fate of Peter Nonay.

Now Peter Nonay was the conductor or guard on an omnibus which passed along the street below our nursery, which we overlooked before it was built up, and we thought him a very cross man. Jenny Finlayson the cook came in at this moment, and heard Mary's story. "Dinna fin' faut wi' the bairn, it's a' true, for it's in the Bible", said she. And if you, dear Isobel and Leslie, read in the book of Numbers 15.32., you will find the original of your mother's little story, though why she fixed on Peter Nonay as the hero of her tragedy I do not know.

We were dearly loved and watched over by our Mother and Nurse Margaret, but neither of them lavished endearing expressions upon us; when they did these expressions were highly prized. "Shut the door, dear," Mother said one day. Now I ought to have done it, being nearest the door, but I waited; and Mary jumped up, and shut it. "Thank you, darling," said Mother. "O, if I had known you would have said that, I should have done it myself," said I, nearly crying. Another time when Mother did something for me, I said "Thank you, Mamma dear." "You said "dear" to Mamma!" said Mary, quite shocked at what seemed a too familiar address. I remember I blushed, but Mamma said comfortingly she thought it very nice to say so, and she liked to hear it.

Tibbie was my nursery name, it being the Scotch pet name for Isabella; but when I was cross, Nurse Margaret used to say, "Ugh, ye Girnie-go-gibbie the cat's guid mither-in-law." She gave us little slaps and shakes sometimes, and kept a pair of leather tawse which she once ostentatiously held in the flame of the fire to make them harder, with the avowed attention of whipping us with them if we were desperately naughty. But this was only a threat, we never were whipped by our dear Nurse. She kept by her an old tartan frock, which she called our disgrace frock, to be put on when we went down to dessert if we had transgressed. I remember seeing sweet Moll, go slowly down the long nursery stairs, so attired, weeping as she went, I with her, weeping for loving sympathy. But I think this only once happened.

MARY'S PRETTY WAYS

Mary used to fidget at teatime so Nurse Margaret made her stand on her little chair before the tea table. Of course if she fidgeted, she fell off, so she learnt to be still. She had such pretty little ways. When she wanted more bread, she would say to Nurse Margaret, "Um mo' bad, I peese, my bonnie dearie." And when she had had enough, "Not um mo' bad I peese, my bonnie dearie" - a pretty little bit of politeness never forgotten, and which charmed Maggie Munro our cousin when she visited our nursery. She could not pronounce R properly, and had to go through many exercises before she left off calling herself Maly Light, "Ruglen lums reek bonnie", (Rutherglen chimneys smoke bonnie)" was what Nurse Margaret made her say. Papa enforced, with much laughter at her efforts, "round the rugged rock, the ragged rascals ran." Most difficult things to say in any case!

She was a tender hearted, shy little thing, and once at Calder Park when at dinner she had been forgotten, she was observed shedding quiet tears before her empty plate. Never would have it occurred to her, or to me either, to have asked for anything, so shy and retiring were we. When she was very tiny she ran in to the dining room at St Vincent Street and kissing the round cushion, said "my dear home"! We had just returned from the seaside. "Eh, the dear bairn", said old Jenny Finlayson, "the dear, warm herted bairn." But I looked on and wondered! For I was a regular country bird and hated a town, partly, I suppose, because I was always more or less ailing in Glasgow, and rarely out of doors all winter, very often too in bed, and Dr Rainy was a constant visitor. He used to look at me nestled among the pillows, and say, "Bye, birdie, in a boggie, Doon amang a wee pickle foggie." Fog is a Scottish word for moss.

The fog-house at Livelands was a charming summer-house made of wood, fir cones in a marvellous pattern, and moss, otherwise fog. I had a great deal of dear Mother's company during the winter afternoons while the others were out walking, and she came to the nursery to sit with me, and very happy I was. She read aloud to me, humouring me in my love of poetry, and reading the same piece again and again. Some of these pieces I can repeat still. She also taught me all sorts of needlework, knitting, and crochet. We were always taught to be useful. Nurse Margaret was a dragon about tidiness, and made us helpful. She taught us to make the beds, the porridge, to fold our clothes neatly, and woe betide her who kept an untidy drawer or cupboard.

Of toys we had few, compared with what children now have. Mary had a doll she called Alabama, and mine was Susan. These names came from an old song, "Oh Susanna, don't you cry for me, I'm going to Alabama, with my banjo on my knee"! Besides these, we had two dolls with china heads, and pink kid bodies; Mary's was Louisa, and mine was Alice Maude Mary after the two young princesses, as they were dressed in little pink cotton frocks, exquisitely made by Mother's dainty fingers. They still repose in the little old chest of drawers, and you, dear children, have often played with them. Louisa has a rather browner complexion than her sister. Dear Alice and Louisa! how many loving kisses have I pressed upon your unresponsive china faces! How beautiful I thought your staring blue eyes, how sweet your unchanging smile! Your destination in years to come, may probably be the dust heap, but as long as I live you shall remain where you are. What imaginations I cherished about you, what mother-love I gave you! How real you were to me! I loved you then in what I considered your incomparable beauty; and, old, and shabby, and soiled, I love you still!

In the same little old chest of drawers, which belonged to Aunt Christian Jane Murray at Livelands, is a tiny straw box with a glass lid, and inside lies in cotton wool, a little wax doll, oddly made, which belonged to Aunt Mary

Wright, Calder Park, and was cherished by her. After her death in 1857, this curious little thing was given to Mary, and our aunts said it was then more than 100 years old. Dear children, all these little details of our childhood and our poor old toys, may seem almost absurd to you, but as I touch the old things I echo Mrs Browning's lines:-

> *"The least touch of their hands in the morning,*
> *I keep it by day and by night,*
> *Their least step on the stair, at the door,*
> *throbs through me, though ever so light,*
> *Their least gift which they left to my childhood,*
> *far off, in the long ago years.*
> *Is now turned from a toy to a relic,*
> *and seen through the crystals of tears."*

Mother and Miss Telford used to say how they never quite knew how I learnt to read, and that I, as soon as I knew the alphabet and word sounds must have taught myself, because just at that stage I was ill, and had no regular lessons. Certainly I never recall being taught to read, but I always remember as I lay in bed, or sat in my little chair by the fire, that I had a book in my hand, and tried to read to myself the story Mother had just read to me. Very pleased and proud was I when Nurse Margaret laboriously wrote a letter, and made me sit by her to spell the words for her. My only distress was, that she could write! Because I so wished to copy Mother in everything, and should like to have written the letters as she did for her nurse, Jenny McNab. Nurse Margaret was, however, a stage in advance of Jenny.

She was bright and clever and invented little things for our amusement; made, mended, and washed our dolls clothes; and even made little rhymes, which we thought master pieces. Mother being from home, she once enclosed one in Jane Anne's letter.

> *"We are all well, All has gone right,*
> *And I hope it will, For another night,*
> *But I hope you'll come home, Tomorrow night,*
> *And I wish the train, To speed its flight."*

Her sister Ann, who was deformed, also occasionally dropped in to poetry to our immense satisfaction. She wrote of Jane Anne:-

> *"As I was going along Melville Terrace, A lady I did see,*
> *Sitting at the window, Drinking up her tea,*
> *I looked in at the lady, Though she did not look at me,*
> *Sitting at the window, Drinking up her tea."*

Izbel at Calder Park was another poetess, but hers were religious effusions, and really pretty. So, before the days of School Boards, with but very little learning, even the servants essayed the steep slopes of Parnassus.

Another relic in the old chest of drawers, is a little medal with a quaint figure on it, a young girl sewing; and on the reverse "For a good girl." This Nurse Margaret bought in Stirling, and at Livelands hung round my neck, as a reward for extra good behaviour. Surely there was never a child so shy as I! It was agonies to me to wear it, and to hear everyone remark up it. We were shy by nature, and the being always in the nursery, and having no companions naturally fostered the feeling. Our only little friend was Ellison, daughter of Mr and Mrs John Buchanan, but we did not meet very often.

DAVIDSONS OF RUCHILL

The only large party we ever went to, was at Ruchill, a country house near Glasgow, which they rented. It was a mixed party, children and grown up people, a regular dance, at which I think, Nancy Buchanan came out. Papa and Mamma, Maggie Munro, and we two little ones went to it. (Jane-Anne was then ill) and the Ruchill Ball was long talked of by us. Ruchill belonged to the Davidsons, and Mrs Davidson was a relation of the Miss Wilsones of Murrayshall, and therefore a friend of Mother's. I remember her as a very stately lady.

MISS BALMAINO

Another friend of Mothers was a Miss Balmaino. She was quite a character. She wore a complete wig and a marvellous headgear. At dinner one day, a button of the footmans coat caught onto this amazing structure, and twitched it off. "O there's my wig", said she composedly, and calmly put it on. At another dinner party, she was sitting next to a lawyer, whose reputation for honesty was not very high. Toasts and sentiments were still then given after dinner. "Will this do for a sentiment", said he gallantly, "Honest men and bonnie lasses!." "No, no," said she quickly, "that would neither suit you nor me." (She was not handsome). She fell violently in love with someone and offered him her heart, her purse, and her hand. His answer was to the point. "I advise you to give your heart to God, your purse to the poor, and your hand to him who asks for it." As no one asked for her hand, she remained Miss Balmaino to the end of her days.

MISS HANNAH SPREULL

Another friend, especially of Aunt Eliza's was Miss Hannah Spreull. I think she was a granddaughter or a great granddaughter of John Spreull a worthy Glasgow citizen who died in 1722, the last of those who were imprisoned on the Bass Rock in the days of the Covenanters.

BLACK SAMBO

It was at one time the fashion to have black footmen, and a lady, whose name I forget, had one, called Sambo. Mother said his mistress remarked that the plate was not quite clean. He took it, licked it, rubbed it on his woolly head and placed it before his mistress again! What may not have been done in Sambo's pantry! He was, however, a long time with this lady; and when he was leaving her, she gave him a gold watch chain as a remembrance. "What for Missis give me dat?", asked Sambo modestly. "To remember me by", said she. "O, Missis, Sambo nebbur forget you"! "Why?" said she greatly pleased. "O because you always scoldy, scoldy on the lasses!" It was true! She did always "scoldy, scoldy on the lasses"! I think it was a remark of the same lady's that we were never tired of getting Nurse Margaret to repeat, because of her amazing imitation of what she called the lady's "clippit" English, "When I was in the Indies, I rode on my horse, with my whip in my hand, and my black fellow running behind, with my reticule over his arm, in this fashion, you know, ma'am."

"SWEETIES"

The dainty chocolate drops and delicious sweets of the present day were unknown in these days; we crunched barley-sugar, "black man" (a stick of liquorice) and there were packets of "mixed sweets", which consisted of almonds encased in smooth, hard sugar, white or pink round sugar wafers called "white-faced lambkins", or "pink-faced lambkins", and a curly kind, "curly-tailed lambkins." The small packet cost one shilling, and kind old Mrs Macnaughton of Glen Park Greenock, often gave us one. We also nibbled with delight, rabbits made of hard paste and water with currants for eyes, and horses of the same stuff. A sort of oblong, hard ginger bread called "parlies", short for "parliament cakes" was also relished. But fine things, we knew not; and our nursery meals were of very plain fare. The packets of "mixed sweets" were called by Mrs Macnaughton "comfits", (no doubt she meant French "confits") but I imagined the word came from comfortable, and certainly found "comfits", very comforting. When Jenny brought us little offerings in the way of rabbits or sweeties, she used to make us guess in which hand she held them, saying "Nievie, nievie, knick, knack, which haun' will ye tak?" We answered, tapping each of her closed nieves (clenched hands) "I'll neither tak' this, nor that, but bonnie Nievie, Knick Knack", the hand on which "Knack" came, being the one chosen. "Loof" meant the palm of the hand. The village of Crossmyloof derives its name from Queen Mary's exclaiming "By the cross in my loof", etc.

MRS MACNAUGHTON

Mrs Macnaughton was a frequent visitor to our house, and a most kind friend to us little girls. Never did she come to stay, without bringing some pretty gift as well as the comforting comfits. She died on March 17. 1868. In Feb. 1868, when Mother, Mary, and I were visiting her son Peter and his wife in Glasgow, we went with Mrs Peter to see our old friend at Glen Park. She was near her end then, but she recognised Mother and was pleased. They spoke of old Cowie days, Livelands, and of the changes in Stirling. "So many of the people", Mother said to her, "are", she was just going to say "dead", but changed to "away", (as Janet the faithful maid had whispered, "Don't

Stirling Interior by Sir George Harvey (1806-1876), "The Lost Child Restored."
Note the black servant in the doorway. Stirling Smith Art Gallery and Museum

speak of death, she can't bear it"). "I wonder at people leaving Stirling, it is such a beautiful spot; where have they gone, my dear?", said the quavering old voice, from the heavily-curtained four post bed. "O", said Mother, seeing another warning sign from old Janet, "They have gone to, - well, - different places!" A quick-witted reply that caused Mrs Peter, Janet, Mary and me to retire behind the curtains convulsed with surpressed laughter.

IN THE COW'S PARK AT LIVELANDS

We paid many happy visits to Livelands. To town hating country-loving me, I cannot tell you, dear children, half the joy of that dear old place. Alas! That it should have been so sadly spoilt by feuing! In the Cow's Park, where Brentham Park in vulgar pretentiousness now stands, I received my first idea of the goodness and greatness of God in nature. We had all three played there one long, sunny afternoon. What immense length the day seemed then, how far a distance between getting up and going to bed! Mother in a Victorian tartan shawl (which we still have), and Nurse Margaret were with us, sewing busily; and, tired out, I sat down beside them, a very little thing, in lilac cotton frock, brown holland loose jacket, large poke-sun bonnet and black cloth buttoned boots. My little soul drank in the beauty of the scene, the marvellous lights and shades on the Ochills, the winding river, the sunny Carse. I could not put into words what I felt. I cannot, even now.

THE DAWNING LOVE OF NATURE

But I know that never in after years did I look from the same field at that most lovely view, without thinking of that day when God seemed to waken in my heart that great love of Nature which has proved such a joy to me all my life; and even in sorrowful days has caused me to whisper to Him (albeit, perhaps, the grandeur and the beauty have been viewed "through the crystals of tears",

"Thou, Lord, hast made me glad through Thy works, and I will rejoice in giving praise for the operations of Thy Hands." Ps: 92.4. Prayer Book 5.

INDEX

Illustrations are in **bold type**

134

Sunday evenings 122
superstitions 16, 18, 60, 121
Sutherland, Mrs ("Lady Woodie") 5-6
sweeties 26, 106, 128
Sym, Isabella 11
Sym, Menie 11

T

tablecloth 23, 40, 61, 73
Tandlemuir 107
tea 15-16, 65, 67, 79, 82, 120
thumb twirling 66-67
tocher 22
Torbrex xiii, xvii, 93
Touch xvii, 8-9, 10
toys 20, 34, 125-127
twins 63, 97
Two Brooms 36

V

Valley Cemetery 8
Victoria, Queen
        as a princess 54
        at Invertrossachs/her shortbread maker 51
        visits Scotland 88
        visits Stirling 90
        Lady Flora Hastings scandal 68
Vittoria 32

W

Wales, Prince of 61
Walker, James 107
Wallace, William 56
Waterloo 14, 32
wasp's bike 12
wedding cake 83
wedding presents 40, 84
Wellington, Duke of (Arthur Wellesley) 31, 53-54
wells, 16
Welsh, Jenny 8-9, 11, 23, 54, 86, 97, 103
Wesley, Charles 62
Westerlands 27
West Indies 20, 40
whooping cough 18, 103, 105
wincey 14
Winchelsea, Earl of 53-54
Wilson, Margaret (of Bourtrees and Netherhouses) 59
Wilson, William 18, 59-60, 61, 91
Wilsone, Lily 18, 40
witches 16
Woodend 5, 32
Wordie, Isobel ("Old Isobel", Mrs Alexander Murray) 1, 10, 26, 93
Wordie, John (of Cambusbarron) 1 10, 91
Wordies 1, 5, 10, 47

Wright, Florence 20
Wright, Isabella Murray ii x-xiii, 97-98
Wright, Jane Anne x, 4, 7, 28, 37, 47, **52**, 87, 89, 111
Wright, Margaret Wilsone 94, 107-111
Wright, Miss Hamilton of Broom (Mrs Henderson) 20, 49-50
Wright, 'Pin' 20
Wrights of Broom 20
Wright, William 58-62
Wyles, Eunice iv, xii

Y

Young, George 85

136

NOTES

NOTES

NOTES

NOTES